Ethical and Legal Issues
of Social Experimentation

Editors: ALICE M. RIVLIN
P. MICHAEL TIMPANE

Ethical and Legal Issues
of Social Experimentation

Contributors: Alice M. Rivlin and P. Michael Timpane

Robert M. Veatch

Peter G. Brown

Edward M. Gramlich and Larry L. Orr

Charles L. Schultze

Alexander Morgan Capron

Thomas C. Schelling

The Brookings Institution
Washington, D.C.

HN
65
.E85

Library of Congress Cataloging in Publication Data:

Main entry under title:

Ethical and legal issues of social experimentation.

   (Brookings studies in social experimentation)

   Based on papers and discussions presented at a
conference held at Brookings Institution, Washington,
D.C., September 1973.

   Includes bibliographical references.

   1. Social policy—Research—United States—Con-
gresses. I. Rivlin, Alice M.   II. Timpane, P.
Michael, 1934–   III. Brookings Institution,
Washington, D.C.   IV. Series: Brookings Institution, Washington, D.C. Brookings studies in social
experimentation.

HN65.E85   174′.2   75-26915

ISBN 0-8157-7482-6
ISBN 0-8157-7481-8 pbk.

9 8 7 6 5 4 3 2 1

THE BROOKINGS INSTITUTION is an independent organization devoted to nonpartisan research, education, and publication in economics, government, foreign policy, and the social sciences generally. Its principal purposes are to aid in the development of sound public policies and to promote public understanding of issues of national importance.

The Institution was founded on December 8, 1927, to merge the activities of the Institute for Government Research, founded in 1916, the Institute of Economics, founded in 1922, and the Robert Brookings Graduate School of Economics and Government, founded in 1924.

The Board of Trustees is responsible for the general administration of the Institution, while the immediate direction of the policies, program, and staff is vested in the President, assisted by an advisory committee of the officers and staff. The by-laws of the Institution state: "It is the function of the Trustees to make possible the conduct of scientific research, and publication, under the most favorable conditions, and to safeguard the independence of the research staff in the pursuit of their studies and in the publication of the results of such studies. It is not a part of their function to determine, control, or influence the conduct of particular investigations or the conclusions reached."

The President bears final responsibility for the decision to publish a manuscript as a Brookings book. In reaching his judgment on the competence, accuracy, and objectivity of each study, the President is advised by the director of the appropriate research program and weighs the views of a panel of expert outside readers who report to him in confidence on the quality of the work. Publication of a work signifies that it is deemed a competent treatment worthy of public consideration but does not imply endorsement of conclusions or recommendations.

The Institution maintains its position of neutrality on issues of public policy in order to safeguard the intellectual freedom of the staff. Hence interpretations or conclusions in Brookings publications should be understood to be solely those of the authors and should not be attributed to the Institution, to its trustees, officers, or other staff members, or to the organizations that support its research.

Foreword

The federal government during the past several years has conducted a major series of social experiments—systematic efforts to judge new or changed social policies by their effects on a sample of the population. Such experiments have significant potential value in improving the design of programs intended to help solve social problems, but they also raise serious ethical and legal issues. The protection of human rights and values has always been difficult whenever people are the subjects of scientific inquiry. The medical, biological, and psychological sciences have developed elaborate procedures and guidelines for human experimentation, as well as a complex literature on the subject. But the effects of social policy are more difficult to control, identify, and measure, and no accepted body of moral and legal rules has been developed to regulate the conduct of social experiments.

The growing literature on social experiments alludes, albeit unsystematically, to recurrent problems, such as the risk of harm to experimental subjects, the difficulty of balancing the requirements of scientific validity and dissemination against the often conflicting need to protect the right of privacy and to inform the subjects. Such questions raise others, among them the post-experimental obligations incurred by, and the right of the general public to be informed about, the activities of social investigators.

To address some of the vexing issues of social experimentation more systematically, the Brookings Panel on Social Experimentation, whose members are listed on page xi, convened a two-day conference of experts at the Brookings Institution in September 1973. The participants, listed on pages 181–82, included social scientists who had devoted attention to the issues, government officials and others engaged in the preparation and execution of federally sanctioned social experiments, and scholars who had investigated ethical and legal issues in medical and social research. This book presents the papers and critiques prepared for the conference, revised to reflect discussion during the conference, along with a summary of the discussion prepared by the editors, Alice M. Rivlin (chairman of the Brookings Panel) and P. Michael Timpane. At the time of the conference, Mrs. Rivlin and Mr. Timpane were senior fellows on the staff of the Brookings Economic Studies program.

The editors are grateful for the helpful comments of a reading committee consisting of John E. Brandl, Charles E. Frankel, and Paul A. Freund. Among the contributors, Robert M. Veatch acknowledges the assistance of Marilyn Barnes, Benjamin Freedman, Sharmon Sollitto, and Peter Steinfels of the Institute of Society, Ethics and the Life Sciences; Peter G. Brown is indebted to Gordon Bermant, Grace Dawson, Gerald Dworkin, Edward M. Gramlich, Herbert Kelman, and Joseph P. Newhouse for helpful critiques, to the Battelle Seattle Research Center where he was a visiting fellow while part of his work was done, and to the Urban Institute, where it was begun.

This is the fourth book in the Brookings series of Studies in Social Experimentation. The series, which is supported by a grant from the Edna McConnell Clark Foundation, assesses the usefulness of experiments as a way of increasing knowledge about the effects of domestic social policies and programs of the federal government.

Alice M. Carroll prepared the manuscript for publication; its factual content was verified under the direction of Evelyn P. Fisher; Nora Krasney and Deborah J. DuBourdieu provided research assistance; and Florence Robinson prepared the indexes.

The views expressed in this book are those of its contributors and should not be ascribed to the staff members, officers, or trustees of the Brookings Institution or to the Edna McConnell Clark Foundation.

KERMIT GORDON
President

September 1975
Washington, D.C.

Contents

Members of the Brookings Panel on
SOCIAL EXPERIMENTATION

xi

ALICE M. RIVLIN

P. MICHAEL TIMPANE

Introduction and Summary

In the last several years the federal government has undertaken a series of large-scale experiments in which new social policies have been tried out under reasonably controlled conditions in order to see what happens and how specific features of the policies affect the results. Samples of individuals and families have been offered negative income tax payments, housing allowances, and varieties of health insurance plans. Schools and sometimes whole school systems have been involved in experimentation with performance contracting, voucher plans, and a wide range of new curricula and teaching techniques for young children.

These experiments promise to yield valuable information that will help the government and the public make more informed decisions about alternative social policies. But the experiments also raise new ethical and legal issues that need to be carefully examined. Is it fair, in the name of experimentation, to single out some individuals for special benefits or special risks not imposed on the rest of the population? Does the government have an obligation to compensate those who are harmed by social experimentation? Must consent of participants always be obtained or may people be required to participate in an experiment? What constitutes voluntary and informed consent? Who should consent for children or for nonparticipants who might be harmed by an experiment? Is it legitimate to bribe poor people to participate in an experiment? Should some types of social experiments be ruled out on moral grounds, even if they promise to yield information that would make social policy more effective in the future?

Experimentation with human subjects has a long history in medical and psychological research and has aroused fierce controversy. The horrors of medical experimentation in the Nazi period dramatized the need

1

for codes of ethics to protect individuals, and several have been developed. But these codes have dealt largely with issues raised by small-scale laboratory experimentation with drugs and surgical or clinical procedures. They are not obviously applicable to large-scale field experimentation with taxes, housing programs, or other social policies. The units of social experimentation may be schools, health centers, or whole communities, and both the benefits and the risks to individuals (while not inconsequential) are very different in nature from those that arise in laboratory experiments.

Large-scale social experimentation is so new that the moral and ethical dilemmas it raises have not yet been addressed systematically. Designers and managers of these experiments have not been inhumane or unmindful of the rights of individuals, but they have had no rules to go by. They have had to make ad hoc decisions as problems arose.

The Brookings Panel on Social Experimentation, therefore, felt it could do a service by focusing attention on the moral and ethical dilemmas raised by social experimentation and taking a step toward developing some rules for the guidance of social experimenters. The time seemed ripe for such an effort, for enough experience has accumulated to identify the common ethical and legal issues that arise in large-scale social experiments. Among other things, this experience indicates that good intentions on the part of the experimenters are not always sufficient to protect the rights of subjects. For example, the desire of experimenters to protect the confidentiality of information given to them by experimental subjects will not necessarily protect that information if a court orders it produced for law enforcement purposes.[1] Second, national concern with the ethics of experimenting on human subjects has been running high, especially in the wake of several highly publicized incidents in which it became evident that medical experimenters had made questionable moral decisions. Forty years of nontreatment for a group of syphilitics in an experiment under U.S. Public Health Service auspices, and the administration of placebos to randomly selected applicants for birth control pills in a San Antonio family planning clinic (resulting in several unwanted pregnancies) have alarmed Congress and added to the push for more stringent governmental regulation of research on humans.[2] Concern has been heightened by dra-

---

1. See David Kershaw's comments, pp. 68–70, below.
2. See *Quality of Health Care—Human Experimentation, 1973,* Hearings before the Subcommittee on Health of the Senate Committee on Labor and Public Welfare, 93 Cong. 1 sess. (1973).

matic psychological experiments on the human capacity for violence involving deception of the subject,[3] and by behavior modification experiments in correctional institutions involving carefully engineered sequences of behavior, reward, and penalty designed to improve the conduct of prisoners.[4] Concern over alleged abuses has prompted the government to provide some rules. In 1971 the Department of Health, Education, and Welfare promulgated its *Institutional Guide to DHEW Policy on Protection of Human Subjects* (it is now being brought up to date and elaborated). While these guidelines were developed in the context of medical research, there is every indication that they will apply to future social experiments—and, indeed, to surveys as well. It seems high time, therefore, for those concerned with social experimentation to focus on the moral and legal issues they raise and make sure the rules are appropriate and that they do not hamper the acquisition of needed knowledge by imposing unnecessary or counterproductive restrictions.

Accordingly, the Brookings Panel on Social Experimentation asked three scholars, who were not themselves involved in social experiments, to prepare papers on the moral and legal issues of social experimentation. Robert Veatch examined the evolution of ethical standards for human experimentation in medical research and offered some judgment on where these standards could be applied to social experiments and where the issues raised were so different that new rules had to be worked out. Peter Brown, a moral philosopher, focused on the doctrine of informed consent and questioned whether that doctrine could adequately protect the rights of certain groups that might be placed in jeopardy by future social experiments. Alexander Capron examined the legal issues raised by social experimentation, especially the constitutional problems of due process and equal protection. Subsequently, Charles Schultze of Brookings and Edward Gramlich and Larry Orr, both of whom had been closely associated with experiments while at the Office of Economic Opportunity, volunteered to produce papers from their own perspectives. In September 1973 the Brookings Panel brought together a group of scholars to discuss the issues raised in these papers. Participants in the day-and-a-half conference

3. See Stanley Milgram, *Obedience to Authority: An Experimental View* (Harper and Row, 1974).

4. Harold L. Cohen and James Filipczak, *A New Learning Environment* (Jossey-Bass, 1971), describes a trial of these notions. Similar programs planned or under way in the Federal penitentiary system have been criticized and curtailed; see Lesley Oelsner, "Behavior Control Issue Unsolved," *New York Times,* Feb. 20, 1974.

included lawyers, government officials, and social scientists, many of them heavily involved in large-scale social experiments. The five papers, somewhat revised, are published in this volume together with comments prepared by several of the conference participants.

The conference did not attempt to cover every important ethical issue associated with social experiments. Issues associated with the professional behavior of the intellectual community, such as honesty of presentation, standards of remuneration, assignment of credit in publications, and so forth, are bypassed altogether. Those related to all behavioral research, such as the protection of individual privacy and the confidentiality of data, and the practice of deceiving or misleading experimental subjects, which crop up in social experimentation but in no special way or in very limited fashion, are briefly reviewed. The focus of these papers is on the ethical issues that are endemic, as it were, to social policy experimentation as compared to other kinds of social policy research: namely, the relationship of the investigator to the subject when the investigator wants to try out on the subject a new policy whose effects are unknown and need to be discovered.

The Balancing of Benefits and Harms

At the bottom of the problems under discussion is a conflict: the benefits of increased knowledge about how social policies are likely to work have to be weighed against the harm that might be done in the process of acquiring that knowledge. There are no right or wrong answers; as the conference discussion clearly revealed, the weights people place on the benefits and risks depend heavily on their background and experience. Social scientists, especially those involved in the design and execution of large-scale social experiments, give heavy weight to the good that can come from more accurate predictions of the effect of policies. They point out, for example, that many people would benefit from the transformation of the current welfare system into a more dignified income maintenance system designed to eliminate poverty. But such a transformation is unlikely to take place as long as policymakers are uncertain about how much the new system would cost and how it would affect working habits. Similarly, housing allowances could ease the plight of the poor and lead to a more equitable distribution of housing, but may not be enacted if uncertainties persist about the cost of such policies and their effect on the supply of housing. The discovery of an effective way of improving school performance of children from impoverished families could bring new hope to many children whose experience with failure begins early in life, while experimentally validated innovations in health care delivery could improve the health and well-being of large numbers of people. Social scientists, impressed with these potential benefits of social experimentation, are nonplussed to discover others who view social experiments as sinister and potentially harmful.

Civil libertarians on the other hand—whether they come from a legal or a philosophical tradition—are always alert to possible dangers to the individual's freedom, privacy, or control of his destiny. They tend to doubt that the benefits of any social experiment justify taking even small risks of invading individual rights. They believe that in the long run, society benefits if it takes pains to safeguard the individual from interference by the state, even where the state appears to be doing good, and they are suspicious of any activity in which individuals are used as means rather than ends.

A second basic difference in attitudes among those at the conference surfaced at several points during the discussion. One group viewed experiments, including large-scale social experiments, as identifiable activities requiring special rules and safeguards; the other believed social experiments were not inherently different from social policies generally. The first group emphasized the uncertainty and possible dangers in, say, an experiment designed to test the efficacy of a new curriculum in a school system and favored laying down stringent rules which any school system would have to follow in undertaking such an experiment. In contrast, the other group felt that most social experiments pose no greater (or lesser) ethical dilemmas than social policies generally. After all, school officials make decisions all the time that involve adoption of new curricula or educational approaches without firm knowledge of what the effects will be. There is always some chance of harm to some or all children which has to be weighed against the possible benefits of the change. Calling the change an "experiment" does not alter the moral dilemma involved or call for special rules. Such rules might have the perverse effect of putting special obstacles in the way of careful examination and evaluation of change, while allowing quite drastic changes that had no experimental or tentative flavor to proceed unquestioned.

The issue is raised directly by Peter Brown, who argues that social experiments are different from policy in at least two important respects: they set up different risks for people similarly situated, and in the explicit pursuit of knowledge they treat the policy's beneficiaries as means rather than ends. For these reasons, Brown believes, the individual subject needs safeguards far beyond those normally provided in the development and implementation of policies. Indeed, Brown believes some kinds of social experiments to be morally impermissible. He would, for example, rule out experiments with children where there was any risk of harm to the child, since he believes that children cannot exercise informed consent and that their parents have no right to consent to their exposure to harm.

Charles Schultze, on the other hand, finds the differences between social policy and large-scale social experiments insubstantial. The benefits of policy are (like those of experiments) often available only to some people; in policy as in experiment, the subject is often free to choose whether to participate or not; and in both policy and experiment, some participants are harmed (even, in a statistical sense, deliberately), yet an increase in general social welfare is clearly the objective. Society has a set of political rules that govern this process—rules it has accepted so far. Except for a few cases (notably that of extreme harm), the political rules of the game are sufficient protection for the freedom of subjects in social policy experiments.

Following a similar line of reasoning, Gramlich and Orr argue that in every social experiment, as in many policies, the government's calculation of costs and benefits is paralleled by the individual's—he sees a positive change in welfare due to the experiment, and thus participates and is free to withdraw. An important distinction must be made, they believe, between the risks that the subject confronts and accepts, and the losses—and gains—that he later realizes. Ex post losses are inevitable, they argue, and should be minimized by design and perhaps compensated where extreme. But these losses do not in themselves pose an ethical problem that is different in kind from the problems presented by new policies.

Alexander Capron added an historical view: policies were formerly designed and installed in blithe ignorance of their possible effects; the invention of program evaluation was a first step to improve this situation, and social experiments are another progression—a way of saying "try out and evaluate the policy before you install it in the first place." This last state is hardly, on its face, less ethical than the first. Thomas Schelling observed that experiments may often be nothing more than field tests, where not a hypothesis but the feasibility of a policy is being tested.

Schelling, however, added a note on which the conferees found uneasy consensus: it is still difficult to define what is a social experiment and what is not, and the ethical principles at stake may be so broad and general as to require attention whenever they may plausibly be raised. In this respect, social experimentation may provide the opportunity, as Rees suggests, to test the ethics as well as the effectiveness of novel program proposals.[5]

Medical Ethics and Informed Consent

Trying out new drugs and treatments on human subjects has played an important role in the growth of medical knowledge. But, as Veatch's paper details, experimentation with human beings raises ethical problems that the medical profession has come to grips with only slowly and painfully. Medical ethics has always concerned the physician's responsibilities to an individual patient (not to society at large). The ancient Greek principle that a physician should "do no harm" still influences thinking about medical ethics. The rise of experimental medicine made it necessary to balance the possible harm to the individual patient of a risky new medical procedure against the future benefit to society at large of having the medical knowledge the experiment would produce. Early traditions left this hard decision entirely to the doctor, but eighteenth-century notions of freedom and individual self-determination brought the patient into the decision-making process. Where a medical treatment or procedure was experimental, a dual requirement evolved: the doctor must believe that the benefits of the experiment outweighed the harm, and the patient must give his "informed consent." The latter requirement was based both on the premise that the patient was the best judge of when the benefits outweighed the harms to him and on the individualistic notion that a person has a right to determine what happens to his own body for good or ill.

Informed consent is by now an entrenched canon of medical experimentation and has been adopted implicitly or explicitly by most social experimenters.[6] The doctrine as defined in HEW's guidelines is the major principle governing experiments funded by the Department of Health, Education, and Welfare.[7] Much of the conference concerned the application of the doctrine and some thorny problems that it raises. Some of these

5. Albert Rees, "Human Values and Experimental Research" (August 1972; processed).

6. But not all. Alexander Capron describes several experiments that the beneficiaries of certain social programs were required to participate in; see pp. 147–52, below.

7. Robert Veatch discusses the doctrine on pp. 23–41, below.

problems occur in medical experiments and some appear to be unique to the newer problem of large-scale social experimentation.

How is it possible to obtain informed consent when the unit of treatment or analysis is an institution rather than individuals? School experiments raise this issue dramatically. Veatch relates that in medicine, modern ethical practice greatly restricts experiments that harm children in any respect, because no one, not even their parents, is deemed entitled to consent to such effects.

School experiments rely for their justification largely on the consent of the institution (that is, the school board) under the theory that the board has the customary authority from the community to make decisions regarding curriculum, staffing pattern, and so forth, and that the risks of an experimental curriculum or staffing pattern are not different in degree or kind from (and are probably preferable to) those that regular school programs offer. Such arguments are sensible, but not airtight. The performance contracting experiment sponsored by OEO, for example, relied principally on institutional consent (with supplemental parental consent), but it is still questionable whether school boards have the authority to commit their constituents to relying on the profit motive in the operation of a public institution.

As Schultze points out, even more serious problems may be raised when the unit of analysis is a private institution, such as a hospital, which has neither governmental status nor any known ability to obtain the consent of its members.

What consent is necessary where there is little risk to the subject? As Peter Brown points out, there are social experiments, like the New Jersey income maintenance experiment, that seem to offer very little risk to the individuals, since all of the treatments are as good as or better than the social program presently in operation. Medical science is not clear on when consent must be obtained. Even during a time when the consent doctrine has increasingly acknowledged the principle of self-determination as an independent criterion, irrespective of the effects of the research, medical associations have continued to hedge on the need for consent with experiments that are generally beneficial to the subject. The devout utilitarians who run most social experiments will need to keep the requirements of self-determination carefully in mind. As Veatch points out, precisely because their experiments offer little obvious harm and because it may be awkward and difficult to obtain informed consent, the temptation to forgo the obtaining of consent will be ever with them. This will, of course, be especially true whenever the investigator also believes that the subjects' knowledge of the experiment may corrupt the experimental results.

How can consent, or a reasonable proxy, be obtained from subjects incapable of consenting for themselves? The three well-known examples of those whose consent cannot be considered valid are children, prisoners, and patients in mental institutions. In each case, medical ethics has confronted unusual problems in deciding the meaning of consent, puzzles that social experimenters could also encounter.[8] The dilemma is: there are classes of individuals who cannot be said to consent meaningfully, and yet there are treatments (such as school, prison, mental rehabilitation programs) that cannot be tested on anyone else.

Either directly or indirectly, children are, of course, the recipients of benefits in almost every social experiment, either as family members or as members of an institution such as a school. Modern ethical theory holds that parents may not consent for their children to experiments that may harm the children, since this conflicts with the parent's obligation to always do what is best for the child. Some ethical commentators might relax this standard slightly, but the strictures are certainly severe. Happily, they may be somewhat less severe in social experiments where the unit of treatment and analysis is the family. Parents will have consented for themselves as well as for the family members in areas (such as bed and board) normally within their purview as family heads. This will not be the case in school experiments, however. There, the problem is deciding whether or not the school board, as a representative body, has the tacit consent of the parents to engage in the experimentation under question. This question could be ameliorated to some extent if the school were a poor school. As Veatch states, "It is impossible to argue that one should not use poor schools for research purposes but improve them instead when the envisioned research is a test to see which policy would improve the schools."[9] Behind this, of course, is the arguable assumption that the children will, either in the long run, or in the short run, or both, benefit from the experiment.

Experimentation with prisoners has long been a problem in medical research, because the freedom of the prisoners is so fragile a concept and

---

8. Issues concerning prisoners and mental patients were not dealt with by the conference in any detail, partly because they were not in any of the social experiments discussed at the conference.

9. Page 44, below.

the likelihood that they will participate in the experiment in return for favorable treatment of some other sort is always so grave. In social research, this danger would remain. When the topic of research becomes penal reform, additional issues arise: if a given penal policy is being experimented with, does the prisoner have the right to participate in it only on a voluntary basis (or further, does the prisoner have a right to participate in it if he wants to)?

In two other respects, however, social experiments may create unusually serious problems for special groups. The first of these is the disadvantaged population. Medical experimenters have just begun facing up to the fact that they perform most of their research on the economically disadvantaged who thus bear a disproportionate share of the experimental risk. In social experimentation, the issue is much more direct. The policies in question are usually intended precisely to benefit the disadvantaged. There is no reasonable way to avoid using them as the experimental group. Difficulties may be reduced, however, if the experimenters obtain broadly based concurrence from groups who represent the poor.[10]

Peter Brown proposes a distinct experimental category for groups whose consent cannot be accepted as valid. He suggests that there may be among the experimental population (especially among the poor) many individuals who have so little ability to comprehend a proposed policy and so short a time horizon that experimental managers cannot assume that these individuals are making the ordinary calculation of costs and benefits that underlies the consent of most members of society. Brown's argument, if followed to the conclusion that experiments cannot usually be done with such subjects, would, of course, seriously cramp the present generation of social experiments on poor populations whose expectations are low and susceptibility to monetary inducements high. But full information is never available; all subjects' understanding of risks will be imperfect. As Joseph Newhouse puts it, Brown "proved too much" and called into question not social experiments but the entire public policy process insofar as it customarily depends on contracts with free citizens. Nevertheless, Brown's reasoning should make social experimenters assure themselves that their subjects do understand the treatment adequately and will not be induced either directly or indirectly by the terms of the experiment into harming themselves.

10. The remaining question might be simply one of political morality, the circumstance where experiments were used, as has been alleged, as an excuse to delay the implementation of policies whose need was already well established.

How much information is enough? Experimental scientists have long tried to steer a course between hiding essential information from the subject, on one hand, and explaining so much of the operation and so many of the remote risks as to either corrupt the experiment or cause unnecessarily high rates of attrition among subjects. These are methodologically serious problems in social experimentation too, especially since there is the possibility of the subject's performing differently because he knows he is in an experiment and because the methodological safeguard of the placebo treatment is not available. The estimation of risks being an inexact science at best, full information is never available to the researcher let alone the subject. Several of the conferees who espoused the idea that individuals should weigh the costs and benefits of consent suggested that *enough* meant everything that the subject needed to know to act in his own best interest. The emerging medical standard, according to Veatch, is that of the *reasonable man*—everything that a reasonable person would want to know should be told to the subject. This standard may be broader than the self-interest formulation; both are a long step beyond earlier positions that the experimenter or his profession may decide on the basis of what is customary practice.

Does a subject have the right to withdraw from the experiment? An essential part of the doctrine of informed consent is the right of the subject to change his mind and withdraw from the experiment at any time. There seems to be little question that social experiments should honor this right. Nevertheless, large numbers of withdrawals would impair the validity of an experiment; a well-informed consent to start with would minimize withdrawals.

What are the obligations of the investigators in connection with the actual harm that individuals may suffer as a result of the experiment? One of the consequences of informed consent is the subject's agreement to the risks of the experiment in advance. The responsibility of the researcher when a risk becomes an actual harm is not clear. Gramlich and Orr with Schultze argue that the calculation of costs and benefits that undergirds the informed consent of the participant means that the investigator cannot be responsible for all ex post harm; and Veatch notes the difficulty, in most social policy research, of attributing a specific harm to the experimental treatment. The consensus was that great risks should be avoided in the first place, if possible, and that there should be some sort of compensation, perhaps through an insurance scheme, for very large, rare harms.

Social experimenters will also need to worry about the termination of their experiments and providing a smooth transition for their subjects into the nonexperimental milieu. For the subject who withdraws from the experiment because he does not wish to participate, David Kershaw suggests that the general obligation is to restore the status quo ante as nearly as possible. But this may be difficult where the withdrawal is occurring precisely because harm has been experienced and claims for compensation may be present. Moreover, as Veatch points out, some social experiments can produce irreversible changes (as when a voucher system is instituted, the previously existing school system or other service institutions change).

What are the ethical obligations of investigators with respect to the control group? Social experiments make extensive use of control groups or comparison groups. The norms of medical ethics are uncertain in this case: sometimes the control or placebo group needs to be informed and sometimes not, depending in part on whether there is any risk involved. In social experimentation, the problem of consent for control groups can get very awkward. First of all, the ability to hide the treatment with blinds and placebos that is present in medicine is not present in social experiments. Secondly, the control or comparison group may be another institution or, in a community saturation experiment, another whole community. Finally, in the usual case where the treatment is benign and substantial, a control group may be relatively hard to secure unless some incentive, subsidy, or other reward is offered. Nevertheless, Veatch feels that there should be some presumption that the control group's consent will be obtained, pointing out that practically speaking the problems of accidental discovery may be more serious than any heightened response or other difficulty that informing the control group might introduce. Kershaw, however, argues that in social experimentation both the treatment and the control groups are randomly selected and that the subjects are then offered an opportunity (and perhaps a payment) to participate and can either do so or not.

A complication would arise, however, if a subject should allege a right to participate in the experiment—a possibility that Veatch sees as an emerging issue and one that will be particularly pertinent in social experiments. In many social experiments, substantial benefits will be available for the participants and, as Capron's analysis shows, there may be equity considerations in law entitling the individual to participation in such benefits. Capron suggests that, in the absence of any other rational criteria, the scientific argument for randomization, backed up by a showing that scarce resources will not allow the benefit to be universally distributed, may protect the research from this claim.

What safeguards are available for persons outside the experiment who are nevertheless affected by it? This issue, which is largely unknown in medical research, arises in social experiments that have large spillover effects. In the course of testing a housing allowance program for low-income families, the entire housing market, including many buyers who have no relationship whatever to the experiment, may be significantly affected. Peter Brown argues that a community's participation in such an experiment is beyond the normal limits of the tacit consent doctrine, under which the locally elected government's consent would be sufficient to establish the consent of residents who are outside the experiment but affected by it. Others hold that such decision is well within the authority of the local government, since that government's decision closely resembles the sort of decision that it customarily makes in accepting or rejecting a proferred program. A compromise view might suggest that very full consent from all conceivably interested community groups, in addition to the local government, should be sought, simply to assure the most stable possible political basis for the continuing conduct of the experiment, as well as a broad basis for consent. That would not, however, resolve the issue of whether compensation is owed to those not participating in the experiment who are nevertheless affected adversely by it.

Protecting Other Rights

There seems to be a consensus that both medical and social researchers should gather only that personal information that is required for the successful completion of whatever research is to be conducted. In addition, the investigator should take continuing precautions that no information revealing personal characteristics will be released to the public. In the latter case, social experiments present some risk. Veatch points out that social science investigators are not now afforded the legal protection that the doctor-patient or lawyer-client relationship enjoys, and Kershaw relates attempts to pry from the New Jersey experimental data private information to be used to further a grand jury investigation. Safeguards of the design of questionnaire and in the coding and storage and destruction of data can all limit but not remove the threat. Kershaw argues for a set of guidelines for social experimentation drawn from principles already

established in law for other confidential communications. These guidelines could be buttressed by a statute that would distinguish the trivial, the
important, and the criminally inculpatory, as well as provide specific procedures for relations between agency and investigator and investigator and
participant.

Another controversial issue is that of honesty. The psychological sciences have, over the past generation, developed elaborate experimental
protocols that depend for their execution on the deception or illusion of
the subject in order, as the American Psychological Association's guidelines put it, "to create a psychological reality under conditions that permit
valid inference."[11] Most social experiments conceived of as large-scale
field trials will not, it seems, have to use this technique. But it is easy to
imagine an experiment in which recipients of some service would have to
be falsely informed that their benefits will be changed or eliminated, in
order to gauge their reaction on some factor important to the policy, such
as job seeking; or to envision a social policy or social experiment involving
participants in planning or some other decision-shaping activity in order
to see how well they perform, without any intention of using their product.

One final unexplored area in social experimentation is the use of unobtrusive measures such as the experimenter's assuming a role or con-
cealing himself (as behind a one-way mirror) or even using concealed or
unobtrusive devices (cameras or microphones). Such techniques, widely
used in sociological research a few years ago, have some obvious attrac-
tion as additional observational and measurement tools in social experiments involving education, penal reform, or any other area where the
minute-to-minute behavior of the subject may be of direct policy interest.[12] The use of such techniques would open new questions concerning
the appropriate definition of informed consent.

The Need for Rules and Procedures

The participants in the Brookings conference found consensus on few
of the issues explored, but they agreed that most of them represented
legitimate, perhaps pressing concerns. Moreover, the conferees found the
existing procedures badly in need of codification. There were, further-

11. Ad hoc Committee on Ethical Standards in Psychological Research, *Ethical
Principles in the Conduct of Research with Human Participants* (Washington: American Psychological Association, 1973), p. 28.

12. See Alan F. Westin, *Privacy and Freedom* (Atheneum, 1967), p. 375.

more, several practical reasons to believe that the requirement for better procedures would persist and grow: First, the scope of regulatory, legislative, and judicial rule making seemed to have been extended, or could soon be expected, to apply to social experimentation. In addition, it seemed on reflection that some ethical issues, such as the meaning of informed consent, might get more rather than less complicated in future social experiments, and that such consent, sensitively and fully obtained,[13] could become a source of methodological and political strength to the experiment, rather than a nagging concern. Finally, in a speculative vein, Alexander Capron suggests that this may be the mere beginning of new ethical obligations for social scientists who may one day soon join their medical colleagues as legitimatized "changers of men."

Professional Standards

The most ancient safeguard of scientists has been the development of objective criteria for professional conduct in research that involves human subjects. Such standards have proved necessary, but not sufficient, for doctors, and they have also been developed in considerable detail by the professions of psychology and sociology.[14] No such code has been developed by the group of persons known as "social experimenters"; indeed, they have no organization that might begin to develop a set of guidelines.[15] David Kershaw suggests as a beginning the establishment of a professional organization.

Peer Review

The primary reaction to the inadequate professional standards for research with humans has been to use peer review in their stead. Peer review has probably been an effective deterrent against gregious research designs in many disciplines and it may have helped establish some minimal levels of ethical awareness, but it is no panacea. The perceptions of a given profession might logically be expected to be somewhat distinctive

13. To the extent, Veatch suggests, that investigators and subjects consider themselves colleagues instead of parties to a contract.

14. Both the American Psychological Association and the American Sociological Association have established guidelines for such experiments; see Jane Clapp, *Professional Ethics and Insignia* (Scarecrow Press, 1974), pp. 625–35 and 733–36.

15. The profession mostly represented, economics, has developed no ethical code in this respect.

and shared, so that its calculation of research benefits and social costs, whether expressed individually or through peer review, would be somewhat skewed, from the point of view of everybody else. And historically, peer review has seldom fulfilled its assumed role. Bernard Barber has noted that rarely, if ever, have such groups actually rejected or significantly changed proposals presented to them.[16] After all, there is logrolling among scientists.

Henceforward alerted, social experimenters might do a better job of peer review, but other steps would strengthen the process:

EXPANDING THE MEANING OF "PEER." The HEW guidelines already suggest that peer review panels should be multidisciplinary and include, for example, theologians and philosophers, as well as assorted scientists. The character of social experiments seems to call for such breadth of view. It should also be extended to include practitioners of the policy in question (such as social workers, teachers, practicing physicians).

Schelling and Veatch suggest that peers in a social experiment should also include representatives of the subjects—poor people, parents, health insurees, and their like.

ESTABLISHING APPEAL PROCEDURES. It is characteristic of the social experiments mounted so far that they extend over a considerable yet definite period of time. This raises the possibility that during the experiment, subjects can be treated, or think they are treated, unfairly or otherwise unethically, or that they may afterward lodge claims against the experiment for harm done. In either case, the courts may be theoretically equipped to adjudicate, but it seems to make more sense that the experiments themselves provide for review and appellate processes that can prevent, mediate, and otherwise lessen such problems.

Even in the best circumstances, few of the conferees would put their sole reliance on peer review or appeal procedures. With the issues only partly defined and the answers in hot dispute, the social policy investigator should expect that his peers' guidance will provide confusion as often as clarity, leaving the burden of ethical responsibility in making decisions on the investigator. In this situation, all concerned may at least profit from a compilation of the questions that should be asked.

16. Bernard Barber and others, *Research on Human Subjects: Problems of Social Control in Medical Experimentation* (New York: Russell Sage Foundation, 1973), pp. 8–9. See also "Experimenting with Humans," *Public Interest,* no. 6 (Winter 1967), pp. 91–102.

A Checklist of Ethical Issues in Social Experiments

The following checklist sets forth questions that prudent investigators might want to ask themselves when planning a social policy experiment.

Is the study really an experiment? Do its proposed treatments or their empirical properties entail uncertainties that are substantially greater than those policymakers usually face in making decisions? Is the decision maker prepared to adopt the experimental treatment as policy, provided only that its expected effectiveness is proved by field tests? Or has the policy already been in effect adopted, for gradual implementation with careful evaluation? (These questions may be difficult to answer, but they will encourage the sponsoring agency or investigator to consider the special ethical requirements of research with human subjects.)

Have you specified and reviewed the benefits and harms of your experiment?

What is the nature of the risk to the subjects? Is it financial or physical, or psychological? How intensive is the harm? How long will it persist? What is the likelihood that it will occur?

Are you satisfied that the expected benefits to society (or, more rigorously, to the subjects collectively) clearly outweigh any risks?

Are any of the subjects at risk special members of society (such as children or mental incompetents) for whom informed consent is impossible?

Have you reviewed the experimental design carefully, to insure that no unnecessary risks or harms are being offered to the subjects? What design strengths would be lost if you eliminated the ethically questionable features of the experiment?

On the other hand, are you sure that the apparent risks are, in fact, contingent on the experiment, or might the subject face them otherwise?

Have you defined the possible risks or harms that may occur at or after the termination of the experiment but to some degree because of it?

In designating individuals for inclusion in or exclusion from the experiment have you used either fair or at least scientifically defensible (for example, randomized) procedures? In addition, will the subjects and the public understand that your procedures are fair or necessary in order to insure their continued participation and support?

Have you obtained their voluntary informed consent?

Have the experiment's purposes and likely effects on each individual been explained to the individual? If the unit of analysis or variation is an institution, are you certain that the institution has the authority to consent for its population?

If you are dealing with special populations, have you analyzed the consent to assure yourself that it is informed? If you are dealing with uneducated or impulsive populations, how have you checked to be sure that the population does indeed comprehend the costs and risks of the experiment? If you are asking the subjects to make kinds of decisions they may be unaccustomed to (such as those requiring long-term versus short-term tradeoffs), are you satisfied that you have not unwittingly misled them?

If special populations (poor neighborhoods or minorities, for example, or disabled children) are subjects, have you consulted with representative community groups to obtain both consent and support for the experiment?

Are you confident that, in the nature of the proposed treatment and in the manner of presentation of the risks and benefits to the subject (especially dependent persons, like prisoners and welfare recipients), you have not offered an inducement, such as a substantial amount of money, for example, that strongly tempts the subject not to act in his own long-run best interest?

If substantial risks are to be faced, will they somehow be compensated for by the experiment? If your experiment offers no return to the status quo ante, or if your experiment could result in some rare, unforeseen catastrophe to an individual, do you plan to insure or indemnify the subject?

Is the subject assured of the right to withdraw at any time during the course of the experiment? If he withdraws while adversely affected, do you have plans to compensate him?

If yours is an experiment in which there is no harm but only differential levels of benefit, have you nevertheless decided to obtain informed consent? If not, why not?

Is there any risk to nonsubjects of the experiment?

Are the control groups or comparison groups in any sense placed at risk by the experiment? Do they know that they are in the control group? If so, have they consented to be in the control group?

Is there any risk to populations outside of the experiment entirely? If the extraexperimental effects are at community level, how has the consent of the community been obtained? If ordinary instruments of government have issued the consent, are you confident that they are so empowered? If some groups within the community are affected more adversely than others, have you sought the consent of their particular representative community groups?

Have you observed the ordinary ethical canons of social research? If you have withheld the truth, or plan to engage in secret observation of subjects, have you fully justified the practice?

In your experimental design and plans for collecting data have you respected the privacy of your subjects as much as possible and established procedures for insuring that their privacy remains protected as time passes? Do you have an adequate legal basis and administrative procedures to insure this confidentiality? To the extent you can legally do so, have you provided written assurances to the subjects of this confidentiality?

Have you developed procedures to maintain the credibility and fairness of the experiment as it goes along? Have you obtained the consent of every party or institution that may reasonably claim the right to grant or withhold consent? Have you specified and carried out a thorough, impartial review of all ethical questions associated with the experiment and provided for further reviews during the course of the experiment? Have you developed and installed appellate procedures by which the subjects may raise issues of fairness, privacy, and so forth, during the course of the experiment?

In all dealings with those involved with the research, is your conscience clear?

ROBERT M. VEATCH

Ethical Principles
in Medical Experimentation

Conscious and systematic experiments "designed to yield results useful in the formulation of public policy, where this intervention involves a sample of the human population and sometimes a control group,"[1] are a very new kind of social experimentation. This research in social policy raises many moral issues common to medical research; thus the established tradition of medical ethics may offer guidance to social policy researchers. Several normative principles for human experimentation are currently generally accepted in medical research. These can be analyzed for their implications for social policy experimentation. In a number of areas, controversy over unsettled themes may point to hazards important to the ethics of social policy research.

The moral principles of medical ethics of experimentation cannot, of course, be applied directly to social policy research. Indeed, the medical profession often claims that its ethical norms are unique, that only members of the profession can know and live by them, that this special professional ethic is not capable of being justified in universal ethical principles.[2] Others argue that the private ethical positions of a professional group should not be morally binding on nonprofessionals. But medical ethics does not encompass solely the ethical opinions of physicians. It comes also from religious, philosophical, legal, and social scientific sources. It is expressed not only in the codes of the medical profession, but also the guidelines of government agencies (for instance, the Department of Health, Education, and Welfare's guidelines for human experi-

1. This is Peter Brown's definition; see p. 79, below. The term *social policy experimentation* differentiates our subject from the more general experimentation in sociology and psychology.
2. See Robert M. Veatch, "Medical Ethics: Professional or Universal," *Harvard Theological Review,* vol. 65 (October 1972), pp. 531–59.

mentation) and religious bodies (such as the Ethical and Religious Directives for Catholic Hospitals), and the writings of individuals in other disciplines. The ethical issues in the field of medicine may overlap with those in social policy research. Researchers in the newer field may be able to learn from the tradition of medical ethics.

History of the Ethics of Medical Experimentation

The controlled medical experiment, designed to gain information rather than to try out a new therapeutic regimen, is a relatively modern phenomenon, one which is customarily attributed to William Harvey's publication of research on the human circulation in 1628.[3] Until a clearly differentiated concept of the medical experiment emerged in the nineteenth century, the ethics of medical experimentation was a part of medical ethics more generally. Certainly the Hippocratic or Galenic physician experimented as part of his medical assistance to the patient, but neither the Hippocratic Oath, Maimonides, nor other prenineteenth century medical ethical compilations mention special ethical obligations for experimentation. The Hippocratic physician's duty is to use measures according to his "ability and judgment" for the benefit of his patient and to abstain from whatever is deleterious or mischievous.[4] Presumably this general ethical norm was thought adequate for regulating attempts to benefit the patient by trying out some new procedure or treatment.

The modern period brought two developments necessary for a distinct ethic of medical experimentation. First, scientific rationalism permitted the systematic design of research giving rise to the differentiation of medical experimentation where the primary objective is the accumulation of knowledge. This requires a new ethical perspective, for, by definition, patient benefit is not the sole consideration.

Second, Western individualism created an intellectual climate challenging the older paternalistic norm of the physician's duty to do what *he thinks* will benefit the patient. The ethical value of human freedom is at

3. See Henry E. Sigerist, *On the History of Medicine* (MD Publications, 1960), pp. 184–92.

4. Contemporary folk ethics of the medical profession often uses two slightly different summarizing norms: "first of all do no harm" and "above all preserve life." These have somewhat different ethical implications in certain contexts but for our purposes can be subsumed under a focus on maximizing benefit or minimizing harm to the patient as the classical ethical normative system of medicine.

the root of the political philosophy of the contract and the evolution of the contract as a major legal basis for organizing relationships among people. From it comes the principle of informed consent, which has recently emerged to compete with the older principle of patient benefit. While this doctrine of consent rooted in individual liberty has been evolving over the last two centuries, it only became a dominant theme after the Second World War so dramatically exposed the weaknesses of an experimental ethic based on social utility.

Ethical Principles for Human Experimentation

The Department of Health, Education, and Welfare's regulations on the protection of human subjects provide a convenient summary of the present consensus regarding the ethics of medical experimentation.[5] The department's guidelines establish principles for institutional review which must be conducted for any HEW-funded research involving human subjects. More than seven hundred and fifty major research institutions in the United States have voluntarily agreed to comply with the HEW guidelines in review of all research conducted in their institutions, whether HEW funded or not.

The guidelines specify three criteria for acceptable experimentation: The risks to subjects must be so outweighed by the sum of the benefits to the subjects and the importance of the knowledge to be gained as to warrant a decision to allow the subjects to accept these risks. The informed consent of subjects must be obtained by methods that are adequate and appropriate. The rights and welfare of the subjects must be adequately protected.[6]

5. "Protection of Human Subjects," *Federal Register,* vol. 39, no. 105, pt. 2 (1974), pp. 18914–20. New regulations have been proposed for protecting fetuses, abortuses, pregnant women, prisoners, and the mentally disabled (see *Federal Register,* vol. 38, no. 221, pt. 2 [1973], pp. 31738–49, and vol. 39, no. 165, pt. 3 [1974], pp. 30648–57); they are scheduled to become policy after a period of time for criticism. Also, Congress in H.R. 7724 mandated a Commission for the Protection of Human Subjects of Biomedical Research, which has the authority to develop new guidelines and propose to Congress ways of extending its jurisdiction beyond HEW-funded research, but for the interim would apply guidelines almost identical to the present HEW policy.

6. U.S. Department of Health, Education, and Welfare, Public Health Service and National Institutes of Health, *The Institutional Guide to DHEW Policy on Protection of Human Subjects,* DHEW Publication (NIH) 72-102 (Dec. 1, 1971), pp. 5–7.

Favorable Ratio of Benefit to Harm

The first of the three HEW principles requires that the benefits of a proposed experiment be substantially greater than the risks entailed. The moral traditions of the medical profession support such an approach to the patient, but the notion of medical experimentation primarily for the good of society has not been easily adopted.

PATIENT BENEFIT AND HARM. In the Hippocratic Oath the physician pledges: "Whatever houses I may visit, I will come for the benefit of the sick, remaining free of all intentional injustices [and] of all mischief."[7] While the pledge may seem platitudinous, it is quite controversial. It precludes the physician's engaging in experimentation other than to benefit the sick. It is silent on consent and the rights of subjects.

The normative ethical principles of the Hippocratic Oath and much of medical ethics are consequentialist: the primary moral consideration is the consequences of the individual's action.

The Hippocratic ethical tradition differs radically in one regard from the classical utilitarian position formulated by Jeremy Bentham and John Stuart Mill. It limits the relevant consequences to the one with whom the individual is interacting—in the case of a physician, to the patient.[8] Thus, by implication, any experimenting must be limited to efforts to try out new procedures or remedies that might benefit the patient. When no clearly differentiated concept of experimentation existed, the moral conflict was not serious. But as the concept was extended to help larger numbers of unknown and future patients, it created serious problems.

SOCIAL BENEFIT AND HARM. Medicine has been very uncomfortable with the modifications that have been designed to accommodate research felt necessary and even morally required for the benefit of society. The roots of Anglo-American professional medical ethics are in a code

7. Ludwig Edelstein, "The Hippocratic Oath: Text, Translation, and Interpretation," in *Ancient Medicine* (Johns Hopkins Press, 1967), pp. 3–63.
8. One branch of medical ethics limits the relevant consequences to the prevention of harm (*primum non nocere*). Giving more moral weight to avoiding evil than to producing good has a certain plausibility. We disapprove of deliberately harming one individual, all other things being equal, to produce good for another, at least unless the good produced is overwhelmingly greater. One position in ethics follows Aristotle in giving such special emphasis to the avoidance of harm (W. D. Ross, *The Right and the Good* [London: Oxford University Press, 1930]. Nevertheless, the special emphasis on not harming is inherently conservative in tone. Rigorously following the principle of avoiding active harm leads to avoiding any medical treatment, let alone any experimentation.

of conduct for medical professionals drawn up by Thomas Percival at the end of the eighteenth century. Percival, realizing that the public good required medical innovation, abandoned the Hippocratic route, defending experimentation as of special benefit to the poor—a rather radical contrast to the role of the poor as the primary subjects for experimentation:

Whenever cases occur, attended with circumstances not heretofore observed, or in which the ordinary modes of practice have been attempted without success, it is for the public good, and in especial degree advantageous to the poor (who, being the most numerous class of society, are the greatest beneficiaries of the healing art) that new remedies and new methods of chirurgical treatment should be devised. But in the accomplishment of the salutary purpose, the gentlemen of the faculty should be scrupulously and conscientiously governed by sound reason, just analogy, or well authenticated facts. And no such trials should be instituted without a previous consultation of the physicians or surgeons according to the nature of the case.[9]

Percival was concerned that mistakes could be made. He advises that the peers of the innovator be consulted. There is, however, no hint of a principle of patient consent.

Claude Bernard, using a consequentialist ethical maxim, goes even further: "Christian morals forbid only one thing, doing ill to one's neighbor. So, among the experiments that may be tried on man, those that can only harm are forbidden, those that are innocent are permissible, and those that may do good are obligatory."[10]

The moral commitment to patient-centered benefit still remains a strong principle (in the ideal at least) in the ethical pronouncements of the profession. As late as 1949 the World Medical Association adopted an International Code of Medical Ethics which contained the norm: "Under no circumstances is a doctor permitted to do anything that would weaken the physical or mental resistance of a human being except from strictly therapeutic or prophylactic indications imposed in the interest of his patient."[11] Then in 1954 the association, without comment on its earlier position, adopted a statement that for experimentation on healthy subjects "every step must be taken in order to make sure that those who submit themselves

9. Chauncey D. Leake, *Percival's Medical Ethics* (Williams and Wilkins, 1927), p. 76.

10. Claude Bernard, *An Introduction to the Study of Experimental Medicine* (Dover, 1957), p. 102. Bernard is not precise in saying that those experiments that do good are obligatory. Those that can be expected to do both good and evil certainly are not. Even those that can do only good cannot be considered obligatory.

11. Reprinted in *Readings*, no. 614 (Hastings-on-Hudson, N.Y.: Institute of Society, Ethics and the Life Sciences, n.d.).

to experimentation be fully informed,"[12] implying that such nontherapeutic research is morally licit. By 1962 in the Declaration of Helsinki the organization tempered its commitment to not weakening the patient except in his interest, recognizing that "it is essential that the results of laboratory experiments be applied to human beings to further scientific knowledge and to help suffering humanity."[13]

Accordingly, the guidelines continued, "clinical research cannot legitimately be carried out unless the importance of the objective is in proportion to the inherent risk to the subject," and each project "should be preceded by careful assessment of inherent risks in comparison to foreseeable benefits to the subject or to others."[14] The Helsinki Declaration merely brought the World Medical Association abreast with the Nuremberg Code.

The decisive test for the consequentialist ethic of medical experimentation came at Nuremberg. It is remarkable that, after the gross abuses of medical experimentation in the name of the greater good of society, rule two of the Nuremberg Code was not stronger. It reads: "The experiment should be such as to yield fruitful results for the good of society, unprocurable by other methods or means of study, and not random and unnecessary in nature."[15]

This triumph for the *bonum communum* defense of medical experimentation is criticized by defenders of the more traditional patient-centered ethic who see elements of totalitarianism in it.[16] Their countervailing emphasis on the rights of the individual research subject is embodied in Nuremberg's rule one, which is more specific about these principles than the simpler Hippocratic ethic centered on patient benefit was.

The ethics of the medical profession has, at least in the ideal, been highly individualistic and patient-oriented. Benefiting the many at the expense of the individual subject has been frowned on whether the issue is human experimentation or health care for those not now obtaining it.

12. Reprinted in ibid.
13. Reprinted in ibid.
14. Ibid.
15. Reprinted in ibid.
16. See, for example, Irving Ladimer, "Committee on Re-Evaluation of the Nuremberg Experimental Principles," in Irving Ladimer and Roger W. Newman, eds., *Clinical Investigation in Medicine: Legal, Ethical, and Moral Aspects* (Boston University Law—Medicine Research Institute, 1963), p. 141; Henry K. Beecher, *Research and the Individual: Human Studies* (Little, Brown, 1970), pp. 232–33; and Paul Ramsey, *The Patient as Person: Explorations in Medical Ethics* (Yale University Press, 1970), p. 26.

This contrasts radically with the moral mandate of a governing body that might be conducting social policy research. Governing bodies are established to serve the general welfare. The deeply entrenched moral priority of patient benefit that has acted as a check on human experimentation in medicine is not only absent, but directly rejected in the moral mandate of social policy researchers. Whereas the codes of medical experimentation grudgingly consent to legitimate medical research primarily for the good of society, a counterethic dominates the moral tradition in medicine. This check is present in governmental social policy research only insofar as the government incorporates within its charge the protection of the individual and his freedom. And governments are unlikely to voice the vicious indifference to the general welfare claimed with pride by the medical profession.

Social policy research may also differ from medical research in the nature of the harms done. David Kershaw points out that the long-range benefits and harms of social policy research are extremely difficult to predict; he proposes limiting considerations of benefits and harms to the short term. This is a classical problem in utilitarian theory that medical researchers also ought to face. The utilitarians, well aware that long-term consequences were difficult to predict, corrected their formulas by giving relatively little weight to more uncertain consequences. A flat ban on long-range considerations is not justified, however. Considering all envisioned consequences, with long-range consequences suitably discounted, seems preferable to an outright elimination of those more distant. Of course the researcher is not responsible for warning of completely unpredictable consequences, although he might be obligated to point out that some unpredictable harms could occur.

An ethic for social policy experimentation will at minimum have to pay stringent attention to the additional moral principles designed to protect the individual's freedom and rights. It may even be necessary to modify the consensus in the ethics of medical experimentation to prohibit experiments where some subjects can be expected to be worse off (presumably with proportional gains to the society) as a result of an experiment. Whereas in medicine it is now considered ethically acceptable for a consenting subject to accept risks for the good of society, two factors militate against this in social policy research: the lack of the subject-centered ethical bias of the researchers' tradition, and the extreme difficulty of gaining consent of all participating subjects when the research is likely to affect children, the senile, and others not capable of consenting.

Voluntary and Informed Consent

The second of the three HEW criteria requires that when subjects are "at risk," they must give "informed consent" to participate in research.[17] The doctrine has been recognized only slowly and for ambiguous reasons. The physician holds a position of great paternalistic authority in the continental "Herr Doktor" tradition. The Anglo-American notion that "doctor knows best" implies not only his right but his duty to avoid troubling the patient with information about his treatment. In contrast, the social contract theory stands at the roots of American social and political philosophy.

The consentual-contractual element, however, was not emphasized in the medical-legal cases of the nineteenth century. These decisions focused on the need to protect the welfare of the individual patient and held the researcher responsible for harm done through his willingness to break with the standards of medical practice.[18]

CONSENT AS AN INDEPENDENT CRITERION. In 1914, a New York decision put forth a clear and independent consent doctrine: "Every human being of adult years and sound mind has a right to determine what shall be done with his own body; and a surgeon who performs an operation without his patient's consent commits an assault, for which he is liable."[19] Not until Nuremberg, however, was this independent principle of the freedom to control what is done to one's body consistently applied to medical experimentation. The *bonum communum* principle of rule two of the code is counterbalanced by rule one's requirement that "the voluntary consent of the human subject is absolutely essential."[20]

Since Nuremberg, consent has dominated the ethics of human experimentation.

THE JUSTIFICATIONS OF THE CONSENT PRINCIPLE. Two justifications are offered for informed consent. The first is summarized by the 1914 court opinion stressing the right of the individual of adult years and sound mind to determine what shall be done with his own body. The natural right to "life, liberty, and the pursuit of happiness" has been interpreted

17. HEW, *Institutional Guide to DHEW Policy*, p. 7.

18. For a selection of these cases see Jay Katz, with the assistance of Alexander Morgan Capron and Eleanor Swift Glass, *Experimentation with Human Beings* (New York: Russell Sage Foundation, 1972), pp. 524–40.

19. *Schloendorff* v. *New York Hospital*, 211 N.Y. 127, 129, 105 N.E. 92, 93 (1914), cited in ibid, p. 526.

20. In *Readings*, no. 614.

to include a right to individual freedom independent of benefits and harms. This means that adults may consent to participate in legal experimentation even if they are not likely to benefit and may possibly suffer harm. For whatever motive—altruistic or self-serving—the individual may consent, provided that consent is deemed voluntary. This also means that even experiments judged harmless (rightly or wrongly) require consent.

Self-determination is independent of a second justification based on the more traditional patient-benefiting principle. It holds that the best way to protect the patient's welfare is to require that he be made aware of the procedures to be carried out on him. Researchers cannot be assumed always to have the subject's interest in mind. Experimentation, by definition, requires a value commitment to advancement of knowledge or benefit of society in general, rather than the simple Hippocratic commitment solely to the patient's welfare. Moreover, in a pluralist society there is a great range of value commitments. No one is likely to know the values of the adult patient of sound mind better than the patient himself. Thus this justification of the consent principle is simply the older Hippocratic principle in disguise—the protection of the patient's own welfare.[21]

The difference between the two justifications is critical—perhaps even more critical for social policy experimentation than for medical. The subjects of social policy research will tend to be large social units—families, schools, hospitals—some of whose members may be incapable of giving voluntary and informed consent or may be impossible to identify and reach because the experiment's effects are so diffuse. Where it is impossible to obtain the consent of all individuals, there may be efforts to return to subject benefit as the basis for informed consent. Then an argument that the subject would benefit more by the omission of consent would justify the elimination of the consent requirement.

THE RESIDUUM OF CONSEQUENTIALISM. The ethics of medical experimentation has retained exceptions to consent on the grounds of benefits to the patient. During the evolution of the consent doctrine some codes required either consent or the benefit of the patient. The British Medical Association approved in 1963 a code specifying that "no new technique or investigation shall be undertaken on a patient unless it is strictly necessary for the treatment of the patient, or, alternatively, that following a full

21. David Kershaw in enumerating items that he sees as important for the subject to know focuses on the utilitarian considerations, providing potentially useful information, rather than items that are simply relevant to subject self-determination; see pp. 65–66, below.

explanation the doctor has obtained the patient's free and valid consent to his actions, preferably in writing."[22] Such a principle applied to social policy research could eliminate virtually any consent requirement since most research would be expected to have some direct benefit for the subject.

The conflict between the two justifications for consent becomes apparent when it is argued that subject welfare actually requires the withholding of consent. Informed consent is often difficult or awkward to obtain, and it is sometimes argued that patients will be harmed if they are given information necessary to give an informed consent. The American Medical Association's House of Delegates in 1966 stated:

> In exceptional circumstances and to the extent that disclosure of information concerning the nature of the drug or experimental procedure or risks would be expected to materially affect the health of the patient and would be detrimental to his best interests, such information may be withheld from the patient. In such circumstances such information shall be disclosed to a responsible relative or friend of the patient where possible.[23]

This opens rather large loopholes in the informed consent doctrine. Communicating to relatives or friends without a patient's permission is also a violation of medical confidentiality. It is an empirical question whether this authority given to the physician to do what he believes is in the patient's interest will in fact protect that interest more than a generally applied rule requiring experimental subjects to give voluntary informed consent. In any case the patient-benefiting exceptions to the informed consent doctrine are incompatible with the self-determination reasons for it. Thus both an empirical judgment about which course is of greater benefit to the patient and a normative judgment about whether the primary objective is the patient's benefit or his right to self-determination will be required in any evaluation of the arguments for the exceptional cases.[24]

22. Reprinted in Beecher, *Research and the Individual*, p. 268.

23. American Medical Association, *Opinions and Reports of the Judicial Council* (AMA, 1971).

24. The courts have recognized the conflict between the desire to omit information necessary for consent on patient-benefiting grounds and the need to disclose to promote self-determination. Their conclusions lean toward self-determination as the overriding moral concern. *Natanson* v. *Kline* and cases cited therein recognize that explaining some risks might well "result in alarming the patient who is already unduly apprehensive and who may as a result refuse to undertake surgery in which there is in fact minimal risk," but they conclude not that, therefore, the physician is obliged to reveal only nonharmful information, but rather that he is required to give full disclosure of facts "necessary to assure an informed consent." *Natanson* v. *Kline*, 186 Kan. 393, 350 P.2d 1093 (1960), the text of which is in Katz, *Experimentation*

The residuum of consequentialism remains even in the current HEW guidelines. For the detailed criteria for informed consent and the mechanisms of review apply only if risk is involved. Risk is defined in a sophisticated, broad way as including "the possibility of harm—physical, psychological, sociological, or other."[25] But to base application of the guidelines on the presence of risk certainly begs for the argument that in some experiments the subjects are not at risk.

The HEW guidelines apply to social policy research funded by an HEW agency or conducted in an institution where all research is voluntarily subjected to them. Since social policy research is likely to be classified as not putting its subjects at risk and since it may be extremely difficult to get informed consent from subjects, social policy researchers might be expected to argue that the consent requirement be omitted. The underlying justification for the informed consent doctrine is, therefore, likely to be particularly relevant.

REASONABLY INFORMED CONSENT. To be adequate, consent must be both reasonably informed and voluntary. Consent may be very fully informed yet involuntary, while it may also be uninformed, yet given voluntarily.

It is literally impossible, an advocate of high levels of experimentation will argue, to get a fully informed consent. This would require transmission of not only endless technical details, but also a lifetime's medical education. Moreover, it is impossible to fully inform the subject since the researcher himself does not know all the answers or he would not be doing the research in the first place.

The "fully informed consent" phraseology is a red herring. No one really advocates fully informed consent because it is impossible, and no one would want it in any case. A better phrase is "reasonably informed consent." According to *Halushka* v. *University of Saskatchewan,* the case on which the HEW criteria are based, "the subject . . . is entitled to a full and frank disclosure of all the facts, probabilities and opinions which a reasonable man might be expected to consider before giving his consent."[26]

The HEW guidelines call for six basic elements of information to be transmitted for consent to be reasonably informed: (1) a fair explanation

with *Human Beings,* pp. 529–35 (see especially p. 534); and *Salgo* v. *Leland Stanford, Etc. Bd. Trustees,* cited in *Natanson.*

25. HEW, *Institutional Guide to DHEW Policy,* p. 2.

26. 52 W.W.R. 608–09 (Sask. 1965).

of the procedures to be followed and their purposes, including identification of any procedures that are experimental; (2) a description of the attendant discomforts and risks reasonably to be expected; (3) a description
of the benefits reasonably to be expected; (4) a disclosure of appropriate
alternative procedures that might be advantageous for the subject; (5)
an offer to answer any inquiries concerning the procedures; and (6) an
instruction that the person is free to withdraw his consent and to discontinue participation in the project or activity at any time without prejudice
to the subject.[27]

Some of these elements are controversial.[28] The Nuremberg Code specifies as basic elements the "nature, duration, and purpose of the experiment"; the method and means by which it is to be conducted; all inconveniences and hazards (in contrast to HEW and the AMA, Nuremberg
specifies the inconveniences); and the effects on health that may possibly
result.[29] Disclosure of the purpose is a particularly controversial element
in social policy research, as is the problem of how much information must
be disclosed.

VOLUNTARY CONSENT. Consent must be not only reasonably informed, but also voluntary. Determinists, whether their bent be psycho-

27. HEW, *Institutional Guide to DHEW Policy,* p. 7.

28. The 1966 AMA guidelines contain a similar list. Neither the HEW nor the
AMA guidelines specifically require the disclosure of inconveniences as well as risks.
In social policy research, inconveniences may be a particularly significant information. The AMA guidelines also do not specifically require disclosure that the patient
may withdraw his consent at any time, although for research primarily for accumulation of knowledge they specify that "no person may be used as a subject against his
will" (AMA, *Opinions and Reports,* p. 12). The World Medical Association's 1954
Principles for Those in Research and Experimentation specify simply that information must include the "nature of, the reason for, and the risk of the proposed experiment" (reprinted in *Readings,* no. 614). The U.S. Food and Drug Administration's
statement of policy and related regulations regarding consent for investigational use
of new drugs on humans is taken from the Nuremberg principle of consent with
significant changes. The FDA regulations in effect in 1966, however, specifically included the requirements that the subject be told that he might be used as a control,
that he be informed of alternative forms of therapy, if any, and that the consent be
obtained in writing (Beecher, *Research and the Individual,* p. 300). The regulations
currently in effect have deleted the reference to inconveniences included in the 1966
version and the Nuremberg Code. This may be a dangerous trend with implications
for social policy research or simply the removal of a redundancy with inconveniences
subsumed under hazards. The new regulations also drop the specific requirement that
consent be in writing; they add the patient-benefiting exclusion by permitting the
researcher to take "into consideration such person's well-being and his ability to
understand" (Katz, *Experimentation with Human Beings,* pp. 573–74).

29. In *Readings,* no. 614.

analytic, behavioral, biochemical, or physical, argue that voluntarism is a mirage, that all "choices" are determined by basic biological drives, early childhood experiences, or the overwhelming force of the relative value of the alternatives presented. Nevertheless, most of us feel that we are able to distinguish relatively more free choices from the relatively less free. The requirement that consent be voluntary uses this apparent distinction.

Medical experimentation ethics has emphasized free or voluntary consent, but has not until recently realized the subtle nature of some infringements on that voluntarism. Not surprisingly, the context for the careful explication of the need for truly voluntary consent is set forth in the Nuremberg Code: "This means that the person involved should have legal capacity to consent; should be so situated as to be able to exercise free power of choice, without the intervention of any element of force, fraud, deceit, duress, overreaching, or other ulterior form of constraint or coercion."[30]

Voluntariness depends on the number of realistic options available. For valid consent the subject must be told of the alternatives available. Some of the theoretically feasible alternatives may, however, be foreclosed because the subject, for financial, ethnic, or other reasons, must make use of facilities where research is likely to be conducted. The heavy bias in selecting subjects from less free groups is a serious problem in medicine that needs to be corrected. But in medicine, for the most part, this bias is not necessary to the research itself. Hence, some have proposed requiring that, except in special circumstances, at least half the subjects be private rather than clinic patients. In research, say, on malnutrition that may require using welfare and clinic populations, special and particularly rigorous review procedures could be required.

By contrast, social policy research is by its very nature concerned with ways to increase the welfare and perhaps the options of those least well off. Those with the fewest options must be the research subjects. An income maintenance or housing allowance experiment restricted to high-income groups would not yield relevant results. Voluntary consent will be

---

30. Ibid. The FDA regulations soften the Nuremberg principle, omitting the phrase "without the intervention of any element of force, fraud, deceit, duress, overreaching, or other ulterior form of constraint or coercion" (Katz, *Experimentation with Human Beings,* p. 573). Likewise the Department of the Army's 1962 Regulation no. 70-25 on the Use of Volunteers as Subjects of Research has followed the Nuremberg principle, but shortened the coercion references, retaining however the phrase "without being subjected to any force or duress" (reprinted in Beecher, *Research and the Individual,* p. 252).

extremely difficult to obtain in most social policy research if that means consent free from the subtle forms of persuasion and psychological coercion.[31]

The HEW guidelines specify that "compensation to volunteers should never be such as to constitute an undue inducement."[32] Compensation is now extremely controversial. The charge is made that low-income groups are coerced into research by bribes of irresistible amounts of money relative to normal incomes and that captive subjects receive inadequate compensation. Compared with medical research, the amounts of compensation offered in social policy research are enormous. When one of the experimental variables is compensation levels, experiments would often include large payments.

Perhaps the concept of voluntary (as opposed to informed) consent must be reexamined. An experimental income-maintenance offer may be coercively seductive to a family with a malnourished baby, as is a request to a father to participate in an experimental kidney transplant for his son who is dying of chronic nephritis. Yet, even if these are psychologically coercive, it is not clear they are immoral. Quite to the contrary, such "volunteering" seems noble and perhaps even morally required. Of course, if it is morally required, then it is not a voluntary action in this sense. What is needed is a new ethical dimension in discussing experimentation ethics. In cases where the offer is psychologically coercive, maybe the legitimacy of the coercive force must be judged. A father's felt moral duty to aid his dying son is certainly more legitimate than, say,

31. Kershaw suggests that it is useful to divide social policy experiments into a program component and a research component. This proposal suggests a radical difference between social policy and medical experiments. In medical research the treatment itself is experimental. It is to establish the effectiveness of the program that the research is undertaken. In policy research, apparently this is not always the case. In some situations it is intuitively obvious that the proposed policy would help the recipients. The experiment is really designed to test the mechanics or administration of the program. If so, possibly the distinction between program and research components is valid. However, in other cases the proposed program itself is being tested. It is not sufficient that a proposed program "would conceivably be adopted as national policy in the future" in order for its program component to qualify for standards of consent applicable to any other governmental program. Rather, the program component would have to qualify in the sense that the recipients actually approve it at that time as acceptable policy. Certainly many programs being tested could "conceivably be adopted as national policy in the future," but in some cases it would require a successful test before that could happen. If, and only if, the program component is known (even by intuition) to be beneficial to the recipients, programmatic rather than experimental standards are justified.

32. *Institutional Guide to DHEW Policy*, p. 7.

the threat of a researcher to expose to the public a minor offense in a subject's past should he refuse to participate in an experiment, even though the force may be much stronger in the former case. The strength of the forces limiting voluntariness must be separated from their ethical legitimacy. Social policy research giving subjects major inducements to fulfill highly moral and altruistic responsibilities will often permit this distinction.

The Principle of Confidentiality

The third HEW principle requires researchers to assure that "the rights and welfare of the subjects are adequately protected."[33] Two major rights are at issue: the right to privacy or confidentiality and the right to withdraw from the experiment.

In spite of the fact that HEW research is primarily medical, the guidelines on confidentiality are oriented to sociological and psychological data. Safeguards should include "the careful design of questionnaires, inventories, interview schedules, and other data gathering instruments and procedures to limit the personal information to be acquired to that absolutely essential to the project or activity."[34] The guide recommends special coding, locked spaces for data, possible ban or restriction on "computer to computer transmission of data," provision for destruction of edited, obsolete, or depleted data, and the eventual destruction of primary data.

The emphasis on social science rather than medical confidentiality may simply reflect the strong tradition of relying on confidentiality in medicine. Medical discussions of experimentation ethics are virtually silent on confidentiality—apparently relying on the ethics of therapeutic relationship. There is a risk here, however, especially since it is necessary to incorporate a new ethical principle—the good of the community—to justify much medical experimentation.

Even among the codes of ethics of nonexperimental medicine there are serious differences on confidentiality, particularly regarding possible exceptions to the rule. The Hippocratic Oath simply says that the physician will not (that is, should not—the normative cannot be confused with reality) "speak abroad" those things that should be kept confidential. This is hardly helpful since what those things are is not specified. Modern codes range from the Declaration of Geneva's blunt statement that "I will hold in confidence all that my patient confides in me,"[35] to the American

33. Ibid., p. 5.
34. Ibid., p. 6.
35. Beecher, *Research and the Individual*, p. 235.

Medical Association's three reasons why confidences can be broken without patient consent: when required by law, where necessary for the good of the community (a principle strangely inconsistent with patient-centered concern), and when necessary to protect the welfare of the patient.[36] The last exception is particularly controversial since it permits the physician to break a confidence when he thinks it necessary, no matter what the patient thinks. This reflects the residuum of the paternalistic principle of the patient's benefit.

In spite of this tenderness of the medical principles of confidentiality, medical research differs in important ways from research conducted by social scientists and other nonphysicians. Not only is there a strong tradition of confidentiality and individualism in medicine, there are in some jurisdictions legal protections of the patient's privacy. With the possible exception of clinical psychologists, researchers engaged in social policy research do not have these protections. In fact, research conducted under government auspices could conceivably be brought under the freedom of information acts. A social policy researcher may not have the legal authority to protect confidentiality even if he desires to.[37]

While social policy research data would not normally be of particular interest to third parties, it could well include information on income, marital relationships, medical and mental testing, and other sensitive data. The proximity of the researchers and their data to government agencies makes the protection of data particularly critical.

The Right to Withdraw from Research

The HEW guidelines provide that the subject must be informed that he is free to withdraw his consent at any time, which means that the researcher gives prior ethical commitment to the right to withdraw from research. The ninth principle of the Nuremberg Code requires that "during the course of the experiment the human subject should be at liberty to bring the experiment to an end if he has reached the physical or mental state where continuation of the experiment seems to him to be impossible."[38] Such individualism, giving the subject the authority to bring the experiment to an end, certainly does not seem applicable to social policy re-

36. Katz, *Experimentation with Human Beings*, p. 314.

37. The Code of Ethics of the American Sociological Association warns that research information is not protected as privileged communication under the law; see Jane Clapp, *Professional Ethics and Insignia* (Scarecrow Press, 1974), p. 734.

38. In *Readings,* no. 614.

search. The World Medical Association's formulation seems more appropriate:

At any time during the course of clinical research the subject or his guardian should be free to withdraw permission for research to be continued. The investigator or the investigating team should discontinue the research if in his or their judgment it may, if continued, be harmful to the individual.[39]

This right to withdraw rather than stop the experiment seems more acceptable.

The right to withdraw raises serious problems in social policy research, however. Large investments are made in any subject, and they will certainly provide a strong incentive to keep the subjects in the experiment.

Even more critical is the question of whether it would be possible for the subject to withdraw. In some social policy research the entire community is really the subject. In a housing allowance experiment, large-scale support of housing costs for one sector of the community would have an impact on the remaining residents. A subject can refuse the particular benefits of the experiment—such as health services or income—but he cannot really withdraw from the experiment.

Moreover, the experiment itself may so change the social circumstances that former options are no longer open. In a housing allowance program a subject's former dwelling may no longer be on the market. Even similar housing might not be available. A serious problem could arise in an educational voucher experiment. The original school system could be destroyed by offering vouchers that parents could use to buy education in any type of school they chose. If a community accepts such a program, an individual family might no longer have the option of withdrawing and returning to an economically and ethnically integrated public school. There can be no right to withdraw in the sense of returning to one's previous life style. Before any such experiment is undertaken, this ethical difficulty must be dealt with.

The Adequacy of Research Design

It is clearly wrong to put subjects at risk in an unnecessary experiment or one inefficiently designed. Four of the ten Nuremberg principles deal with adequacy of research design:

39. Declaration of Helsinki, in *Readings,* no. 614. The principle applies only to nontherapeutic research, suggesting once again that the old patient-benefiting principle might justify continuation of therapeutic research even over the patient's request to withdraw.

(3) The experiment should be so designed and based on the results of animal experimentation and a knowledge of the natural history of the disease or other problem under study that the anticipated results will justify the performance of the experiment.

(4) The experiment should be so conducted as to avoid all unnecessary physical and mental suffering and injury.

(7) Proper preparations should be made and adequate facilities provided to protect the experimental subject against even remote possibilities of injury, disability, or death.

(8) The experiment should be conducted only by scientifically qualified persons. The highest degree of skill and care should be required through all stages of the experiment of those who conduct or engage in the experiment.[40]

Platitudinous in the medical context, these would be difficult to apply to social policy research. In medicine a long tradition complete with governmental protocols exists for the stages of research. Prior animal experimentation works well for toxicology studies but is meaningless for social policy studies. A progression from toxicological (safety) studies to effectiveness studies through carefully regulated geometric increases in sample sizes is clearly established in pharmacology, but certainly not for social experimentation.

The competence of the researchers is more carefully controlled in medical than in social policy studies. While certainly all licensed physicians are not competent to conduct research, limitation of medical research involving humans to physicians sets some minimal controls. In contrast, in social policy research virtually no limits exist other than those imposed by financial restrictions. A study conducted by or for a government agency might use untrained field workers. Maybe for social policy research, special mechanisms such as review committees will have to be established to set minimal criteria for researchers and their agents.

The absence of clear-cut steps for testing a research design prior to experimenting with human subjects in the field is one of the major differences between medical and social policy research.

The Principle of Review

Traditionally in medicine with its individualism the first line of defense against ill-advised research has been a strong appeal to the individual researcher's conscience. The back-up has been a series of ex post facto review mechanisms established within professional medical organizations.

40. In *Readings*, no. 614.

But a study of 404 projects using human subjects at two institutions found that 8 percent were evaluated *by the researchers themselves* as having risks to the subjects not offset by potential benefits to either the subjects themselves or to society at large.[41] Of course, this does not imply that projects evaluated by the researchers more favorably were in fact justified.

The alternative to professional review is public review. Traditionally the public review mechanism has been the courts, but more recently the Food and Drug Administration and HEW have provided opportunities for public preview and review for research involving drugs and all research funded by HEW. The HEW regulations require institutional review of research proposals, prior to approval, by a committee composed of members of varying backgrounds and including persons whose primary concerns lie in areas other than the conduct of research, development, and service programs of the type supported by HEW. The committee members must be identified by name, must adopt a set of principles of review, and must submit initial and continuing review certifications. Although review is beginning to be seen as essential, the nature of the review and the backgrounds of the reviewers are still matters of controversy.

I believe that "peer" review should be based primarily on peers of the subject rather than peers of the researcher,[42] but this is clearly not a generally recognized standard as yet. The value questions at stake are ones where no special expertise resides within a professional group and about which there may even be biases. Researchers as a group certainly have a unique value commitment to furthering knowledge. If this is the case, then peers of the subject would be the appropriate individuals for reviewing the social and ethical (not the technical) aspects of a research proposal. Even if peers of the researcher are the reviewers, there is substantial debate about what constitutes a peer.

In social policy research the question of adequate review will raise new problems. For better or worse the professional researchers involved will not have a strong professional organization with established review mech-

41. Bernard Barber and others, *Research on Human Subjects: Problems of Social Control in Medical Experimentation* (New York: Russell Sage Foundation, 1973), p. 51.

42. See testimony of Robert M. Veatch in *Quality of Health Care—Human Experimentation,* Hearings before the Subcommittee on Health of the Senate Committee on Labor and Public Welfare, 93 Cong. 1 sess. (1973), pt. 1, pp. 265–75; reprinted in revised form as Robert M. Veatch and Sharmon Sollitto, "Human Experimentation—The Ethical Questions Persist," *Hastings Center Report,* vol. 3 (June 1973), pp. 1–3.

anisms. Even if they had such well established mechanisms, they would have no strong sanctions analogous to the medical profession's power to deprive the errant physician of hospital and other collegial privileges. They also lack bureaucratized public review mechanisms. Some research will originate within the HEW sphere or will be conducted by institutions in voluntary compliance with HEW guidelines, but probably a larger proportion of social policy research will fall outside the regulations. The HEW review personnel, who work out of the National Institutes of Health, do not take seriously social and social policy research outside the health complex. Experiments involving housing, transportation, labor, and international affairs (such as population programs funded by the U.S. Agency for International Development) are not covered by the guidelines, although legislation has been proposed to extend the regulations to governmental agencies other than HEW.

The question of who is the proper peer is even more complex in social policy. Except possibly for research under HEW guidelines, there are no indications of what adequate review mechanisms would be. Yet the medical precedent suggests that no social policy research should be conducted until adequate review mechanisms are developed.

The most serious breakdown in the analogy between medical and social policy research is probably in the mechanisms of review. In medicine it has taken many years to develop a concept of systematic review of research design. For decades, medicine stumbled into research programs vaguely aware that there were potential risks to subjects, but not setting up such systematic mechanisms as review committees, guidelines, and governmental regulations to minimize those risks. Social policy research is now where medicine was years ago; perhaps this newer enterprise will learn from medicine's mistakes.

Since the social policy research community is not as well defined, it might not make the mistake of assuming that review could be handled by those within the research community itself. Social policy research may be so different, not only in the nature of the research community, but also in the nature of the questions being asked, the risks to the subjects, and the nature of the subject population, that it would be wise to avoid overly close identification with the medical model. Thus Kershaw's suggestion that a professional society of social experimenters could provide the review could be dangerous. Even if such an organization might serve other purposes, if the American Medical Association is any example, review and discipline should be left to others. Not only is there a strong inclination to protect the interests of the professional community, but there are systematic professional value commitments (such as the value of research data per se) that would necessarily be incorporated into review decisions.

Special Contexts for Experimentation

Several special contexts for research raise special moral problems. These include research involving children, prisoners, mental patients, and special ethnic and economic groups, as well as specially funded research.

Experimentation on Children

Often, research intended for the benefit of a patient is distinguished from that intended primarily for accumulation of scientific knowledge. With competent adult patients capable of giving reasonably informed consent the distinction is not crucial. In research involving children[43] and others incapable of giving reasonably informed and voluntary consent, however, the ethical foundations are different and require reintroduction of the distinction between therapeutic and nontherapeutic research. While the strongest moral foundation for a consent doctrine among adults capable of giving meaningful consent is the principle of self-determination, this cannot be the moral foundation for proxy consent.

Two justifications for proxy consent are possible. First, proxy consent could be justified as functioning to protect the right of self-determination of the guardian. A parent has the right within limits to choose the school that his child will attend, a right that is highly praised. Yet this cannot be the justification for proxy consent in experimentation. The child is not the property of the parent. A parent is not permitted morally or legally to volunteer his child for a risky, nontherapeutic experiment in which he himself could participate and would be praised for his altruism.

A second justification requires reverting to the older patient-protecting principle of Hippocratic medicine. The parent has an obligation to care for and protect the welfare of his child. He will be permitted to consent to his child's participation when it will not infringe on the child's welfare or alternatively when it is done for the child's welfare.

43. On the use of children as research subjects in medicine, see Katz, *Experimentation with Human Beings,* pp. 955–1011; and Beecher, *Research and the Individual,* pp. 63–69. For a series of cases, see M. H. Pappworth, *Human Guinea Pigs* (Beacon, 1967), pp. 31–43.

The differences in these two alternatives have generated an important controversy. They show up in two major codes that differ significantly.[44] The World Medical Association's Declaration of Helsinki is unexplainably unprotective of children's interests. For nontherapeutic research involving legally incompetent subjects, "consent of the legal guardian should be procured."[45] While such a provision is understandable in potentially therapeutic research, unless qualified it is most questionable for nontherapeutic research. The 1966 Principles of the American Medical Association attempt to qualify the terms of research "primarily for the accumulation of scientific knowledge." They specify that:

Minors or mentally incompetent persons may be used as subjects only if: (i.) The nature of the investigation is such that mentally competent adults would not be suitable subjects. (ii.) Consent, in writing, is given by a legally authorized representative of the subject under circumstances in which an informed and prudent adult would reasonably be expected to volunteer himself or his child as a subject.[46]

The first requirement is certainly plausible, but the second still raises problems.

Ramsey argues that the circumstances under which an adult would reasonably be expected to volunteer himself is not an adequate standard. This would be to counsel parents to "do to children always as they would do to themselves."[47] Yet, certainly the child should not be subjected involuntarily to the same altruistic sacrifices permitted and honored in an adult. What an informed and prudent adult would be expected to volunteer his child for is a more plausible standard. Even this, however, begs the question of what it would be reasonable to volunteer one's child for. Certainly what a researcher would volunteer his child for should not be used as a standard. The researcher may subject his child to unreasonable risks for the benefit of research.

Ramsey argues that the standard must be the rigid application of the patient-benefiting principle. The parent has a sacred obligation to protect the child's interest. Thus proxy consent is acceptable only when the child

44. A similar point is made by Paul Ramsey in his important article, "Consent as a Canon of Loyalty with Special Reference to Children in Medical Investigation," in *The Patient as Person*, pp. 19–26.

45. In *Readings*, no. 614.

46. AMA, *Opinions and Reports*, p. 42.

47. "Consent as a Canon of Loyalty," p. 16. Ramsey argues that normally this would be a potentially therapeutic experiment, but in an epidemic, proxy consent for subjecting the child to research on a disease that he does not have could be justified as protection of the child's health and welfare.

is treated as an end rather than a means—when he himself stands some chance of benefit. This rigorous position is supported by Paul Freund who claims that "the law is that parents may consent for the child if the invasion of the child's body is for the child's welfare or benefit."[48]

A position with only slightly different practical consequences, but implying a much different theoretical foundation, is presented by Henry Beecher:

Parents still have the right to decide whether their children will participate in experimentation, even if not for their direct benefit, provided the studies contemplated have no discernible risk and have been approved by a high-level review committee as necessary and valuable for human progress and do not unfairly take advantage of the child.[49]

He differs from Ramsey in justifying research as "necessary and valuable for human progress" rather than for the child's benefit.

An intermediate case is raised by experiments on children where the children benefit, but do so because of their social circumstances. The clearest example is the controversial Willowbrook experiments on hepatitis where institutionalized, mentally retarded children have been given hepatitis intentionally. This is defended on the grounds that the inmates at this hospital for retarded children would normally get hepatitis and getting it under controlled medical conditions is preferable. Probably the most serious flaw in this defense is that it depends on the perpetuation of the substandard medical conditions. The researchers are taking advantage of the poor quality of medical care for research purposes rather than using medical resources to improve the conditions.

The question of children as subjects is particularly critical in social policy research, for the research will almost always involve children in diffuse and indirect ways. Fortunately in most cases it is plausible to conclude that children will benefit and parents will be directly involved and able to give consent for their children. For some experiments, however, the harms envisioned may be greater than the benefits for the children, especially when families are serving as controls. If envisioned benefits for the children appear to be clearly less weighty than the envisioned harms serious, such research would be morally unacceptable.

That children may benefit from social policy research, but only because

48. "Ethical Problems in Human Experimentation," *New England Journal of Medicine*, vol. 273 (September 1965), p. 691.

49. *Research and the Individual*, pp. 67–68. See also William J. Curran and Henry K. Beecher, "Experimentation in Children," *Journal of the American Medical Association*, vol. 210 (October 1969), pp. 77–83.

of their originally unfavorable position, raises more complicated questions. The issue is not precisely parallel to the medical situation where any attention would carry benefits. While it can be argued that there is a more stringent moral obligation to correct the poor medical conditions than to take advantage of them for research purposes, in social policy research the poor conditions may be precisely what the research is aimed at. It is impossible to argue that one should not use poor schools for research purposes but improve them instead when the envisioned research is a test to see which policy would improve the schools. This means that children and others in relatively poor social and economic circumstances will be singled out as research targets, but that there is good reason to believe that they will benefit from the research itself. The counter argument that one should do something directly to improve the social conditions of the research subjects fails in this special case.

Experimentation on Prisoners

The issues raised by research on prisoners differ from those raised in research on children.[50] Children normally cannot provide a reasoned consent, but prisoners are not without the powers to do so. At some point during trial they should have been judged competent to stand trial. The moral imperative of research on children is that their welfare be placed first (or at least not compromised). For prisoners or other competent subjects, personal welfare is not normally the primary or sole ethical consideration.

While prisoners normally do not lack the capacity to offer a reasonably informed consent, their capacity to do so voluntarily is questionable. During the Second World War, prisoners in Illinois were permitted to participate in medical experiments including important work on malaria. A committee later appointed to determine when prisoners may be permitted to serve as subjects and when they may be granted a reduction of sentences as a reward argued:

The most important requirement for the ethical use of human beings as subjects in medical experiments is that they be volunteers. Volunteering exists

50. For a discussion of issues of prison research, see Ladimer and Newman, *Clinical Investigation in Medicine,* pp. 461–72; and Katz, *Experimentation with Human Beings,* pp. 1013–52. Recent summaries of cases include Pappworth, *Human Guinea Pigs,* pp. 60–68; Aileen Adams and Geoffrey Cowan, "The Human Guinea Pig: How We Test New Drugs," *World,* Dec. 5, 1972, pp. 20–24; and Jessica Mitford, "Experiments Behind Bars," *Atlantic Monthly,* January 1973, pp. 64–73.

when a person is able to say "yes" or "no" without fear of being punished or of being deprived of privileges due him in the ordinary course of events.[51]

The coercive aspect of prison research is normally not punishment or deprivation of privileges for failure to participate, but such irresistible inducements as money, time off for good behavior, reduced sentences, and favorable treatment in prison. HEW guidelines specify that "compensation to volunteers should never be such as to constitute an undue inducement."[52] Nevertheless, Robert Q. Marston, while head of the National Institutes of Health, warned of the need for additional protection for minors, prisoners, and the mentally ill:

Any financial compensation to subjects in such institutions would be reasonably related to the amounts paid for other services and not so high as to constitute undue inducement. We would require a clear statement that neither participation in the proposed research project nor withdrawal from it will materially affect the conditions or terms of any subject's confinement.[53]

While the standard of compensation "reasonably related to the amounts paid for other services" is one method of handling the problem of unfair inducement, this deprives the prisoner of one of his few opportunities to earn money.[54] This is another example of research subjects benefiting from research only because of the general social conditions that radically limit their options. The moral legitimacy of this must certainly be questioned. An alternative would be to increase to a reasonable level compensation for other work performed. These problems have led some to argue that persons under constraint cannot be presumed to give voluntary consent and that, therefore, prison research is morally unacceptable.[55]

51. Committee Appointed by Governor Dwight H. Green, "Ethics Governing the Service of Prisoners as Subjects in Medical Experiments," *Journal of the American Medical Association,* vol. 136 (February 1948), pp. 447–58; reprinted in Ladimer and Newman, *Clinical Investigation in Medicine,* p. 464.

52. *Institutional Guide to DHEW Policy,* p. 7.

53. "Research on Minors, Prisoners and the Mentally Ill," *New England Journal of Medicine,* vol. 288 (January 1973), p. 158. In this Marston differs from the Green committee, which endorsed sentence reduction for participation provided it was not "excessive."

54. Recently 96 of 175 inmates at Lancaster County prison protested the moratorium on prison research in Pennsylvania, arguing that the research did not harm them and enabled them to pay off their fines and court costs. *New York Times,* April 15, 1973.

55. See discussion in G. E. W. Wolstenholme and Maeve O'Connor, eds., *Ethics in Medical Progress: With Special Reference to Transplantation* (Little, Brown, 1966), pp. 204–05. A 1961 draft of a code of ethics for human experimentation of the World Medical Association included a complete prohibition on the use of prisoner

Other arguments on prisoner subjects involve the relationship of personal and social welfare. It is argued that expiation is both a moral right and a duty (although its being a duty does not necessarily imply that society ought to extract such expiatory activity). Studies on prisoner motivation include, in addition to more self-serving motives, a desire to "repay the debt to society."[56]

A related but rather strange argument from a peculiar sense of justice claims that if prisoners can benefit greatly from volunteering (in money, in reduced time, or in increased self-esteem), then they should not be permitted these satisfactions. A resolution adopted by the House of Delegates of the American Medical Association in 1952 expressed disapproval of the participation of "persons convicted of . . . heinous crimes" and urged that they be "ineligible for meritorious or commendatory citation."[57] The ethical issues raised by this perspective may be raised again in penal policy research. Since social policy research often will be beneficial to the participants, some may argue that subjects are being unfairly benefited.

Experimentation on Mental Patients

Mental (and for that matter, physical) patients represent another captive research population. Often grouped with prisoners, they are in an ethically unique position. While children cannot give informed consent and prisoners may not be able to give voluntary consent, the consent of the patient is much more ambiguous. Certainly options are often very limited, generating questions about whether the consent is voluntary; but can the mental patient's consent be reasonably informed? The traditional assumption, that the mental patient is incompetent to make such judgments, is being challenged. Courts are now recognizing the right of even an involuntarily committed patient to refuse to accept medical treatment, arguing he is competent to make that refusal.[58] The new competency rul-

---

subjects, but the version adopted in 1964 did not; see Katz, *Experimentation with Human Beings*, p. 1026. For a proposal for a temporary moratorium until adequate safeguards can be developed, see Alexander M. Capron, "Medical Research in Prisons," *Hastings Center Report*, vol. 3 (June 1973), pp. 4–6.

56. Robert E. Hodges and William B. Bean, "The Use of Prisoners for Medical Research," *Journal of the American Medical Association*, vol. 202 (November 1967), pp. 177–79; and John C. McDonald, "Why Prisoners Volunteer to be Experimental Subjects," ibid., pp. 175–76.

57. Beecher, *Research and the Individual*, p. 225.

58. *New York City Health and Hospitals Corporation and Edward A. Stolzen-*

ings may mean that it is legally easier to obtain consent from mental patients, but also that more caution must be exercised in assuring that the criteria for consent and for a favorable ratio of benefits to harms are met.

Experimentation on Special Groups

Research proposals in which subjects for experimentation are chosen because of their social, ethnic, or economic characteristics also require rigorous monitoring. In recognition that the poor—those who use clinics and medical resources of welfare agencies—are used disproportionately as medical research subjects, especially rigorous standards and review for such research are beginning to be called for.

Social policy research involving specially defined socioeconomic groups is more likely to benefit the subjects than is medical research, since it is not always subject to criticism that basic social changes are being neglected in favor of research.

A critical element in gaining legitimacy for such research is community consent openly arrived at. This of course raises serious problems of determining who speaks for the community and what would constitute a valid consent, problems that are being faced in society generally. The most closely analogous problem in medicine is in the establishment of pilot community-wide programs for genetic screening. In pilot programs where efforts have been made to elicit broad-based community support (such as in the Tay Sachs screening program in Baltimore), problems have not arisen; in other programs (including some testing for sickle cell disease and traits), failure to obtain community consent has generated hostility.

Nonfunded and Specially Funded Research

Mainstream, funded medical research is now beginning to receive thorough review. Research funded through less orthodox channels (government agencies other than the National Institutes of Health such as the Agency for International Development and the Defense Department, as well as state and local government agencies and private agencies including drug companies) avoids these review requirements.

---

berg, *Associate Director, Bellevue Hospital, Petitioners,* v. *Paula Stein,* 335 N.Y.S.2d 461 (1972), and the opinion of Judge Alfred T. Williams, June 6, 1973, in the court of common pleas of North Hampton County (Pennsylvania), Orphan's Court Division, In re: The Appointment of a Guardian of the Person of Maida Yetter.

Nonfunded research is not yet generally recognized as raising special ethical problems, yet several such cases have arisen. Prior to submitting a full-blown proposal for major funding, an enterprising clinician may well try out an idea on one or more of his patients. The researcher may not even conceive of what he does as research. Review of such work is not now required by any federal regulations.

In social policy research some nonfunded experiments on a small scale may be anticipated. The problem of specially funded research should be particularly serious in social policy research. Virtually any government agency might undertake it, but none so frequently as to devote special attention to the question of ethics. Some overarching mechanism for review, such as the HEW guidelines, is needed for all federally funded research. Social policy research will be conducted by a large number of agencies and by a highly diverse group of government officials and social scientists. Probably none will have a great deal of experience in dealing with the ethical issues.

Emerging Themes and Controversies

There is a substantial, if recent, consensus on the normative principles of human experimentation. And there is a general appreciation of the special requirements for research in certain contexts. But in a number of areas, no consensus has yet emerged, or the existence of problems is just beginning to become apparent.

The Expanding Concept of Experimentation

Aside from some rather defensive rationalizations that "all medicine is really an experiment," only recently has the breadth and pervasiveness of experimental activity been recognized. For some time researchers have recognized that nontherapeutic surgery, cardiac catheterization, or drug administration constituted research, but only recently have questions begun to be asked about tests on blood left over in laboratories, the addition of a simple pain-threshold test to the routine physical examination (to compare thresholds on the basis of sex, ethnic background, or age), or the systematic screening of urine samples for illegal drug use (to study rates of clandestine use of drugs).

The most significant expansion of the concept of human experimentation is in the nonorganic area. As late as a decade ago, subjects of psychological experiments were treated in a manner completely divorced from the more fully developed medical principles. Deception, experimentation without consent, even compulsory participation of psychology students were commonplace. Sociological research involving standard techniques such as interviews and questionnaires now must meet the same review procedures as medical research. Secret observers and what are called "unobtrusive measures" are now being seriously questioned.

Researcher role-playing may involve potential harms to the unknowing subjects. Warwick describes a study in which the sociologist as "watch-queen" observes homosexual activities for purposes of studying the sociological patterns.[59] Here, potentially incriminating information is obtained. Warwick describes both potential benefits and harms to the subjects in criticizing this experiment. In other unobtrusive studies, however, it is hard to conceive of serious risks. The main ethical criticism is the violation of the subject's privacy.

A few years ago social policy research might have been excluded from the concept of experimentation. Now, however, with the expanding dimensions of that concept, it cannot be. Increasingly, the social scientist, for the protection of his own project and his profession as well as to fulfill his ethical obligations to his subject, will have to conform to consent procedures, review mechanisms, and other devices formerly reserved for medicine.

The Standard for Determining Risks

One of the most significant and controversial new themes appeared suddenly, in 1969. A basic element of an informed consent is the disclosure of the risks of the research to the subject. But just how much of the risk must be disclosed? Obviously, all risks cannot be since the list is virtually infinite. In the evolution of the informed consent doctrine up to and including the decision in *Natanson v. Kline* in 1960, the standard was one borrowed from negligence cases and the patient-benefiting principle. The researcher was expected to conform to the "standard of the profession":

The duty of the physician to disclose, however, is limited to those disclosures which a reasonable medical practitioner would make under the same or similar

59. Donald P. Warwick, "Tearoom Trade: means and ends in social research," *Hastings Center Studies*, vol. 1, no. 1 (1973), pp. 27–38.

circumstances. How the physician may best discharge his obligation to the patient in this difficult situation involves primarily a question of medical judgment.[60]

Thus, if a surgeon slipped and cut a blood vessel during a complicated operation, the court would hear testimony of experts to determine whether the normally competent practitioner would be likely to make the same mistake. Nineteenth century decisions based on the Hippocratic norm of doing what the physician thinks would benefit the patient, likewise, appealed to the standard of the profession to determine whether a procedure "conforms to the system of established treatment." Thus Judge Schroeder held in *Natanson* v. *Kline* that "expert testimony of medical witnesses is required to establish whether such disclosures are in accordance with those which a reasonable medical practitioner would make under the same or similar circumstances." He qualified the standard of the profession, however, saying that "*so long as the disclosure is sufficient to assure an informed consent,* the physician's choice of plausible courses should not be called into question if . . . he proceeded as competent medical men would have done in a similar situation."[61] The level of disclosure must also be sufficient for an informed consent. The question remains, however, how much information is needed for a consent to be informed.

Since 1969 the standard of the profession has been abandoned in a series of new and exciting legal opinions. The older standard was based on the fallacy that special medical expertise is needed to decide whether or not it is desirable to know a particular piece of information before making an informed decision.

The 1969 case involved a patient who had suffered a neck injury in a fall down an embankment. His physicians proposed a diagnostic myelogram. The procedure, described as a relatively simple one frequently performed by physicians, involves insertion of a needle into the spinal column to study the flow of spinal fluid. In this case, injury apparently resulted causing terrible pain, and then after twenty-four hours a sensation of a "rubber leg," numbness and weakness of the leg, and dorsiflexion of the foot, referred to as a "drop foot." No one questioned that the procedure caused the injury or that the physician failed to give the patient information about the risk of this injury. The physician's defense was that no evidence was offered that the standard of professionals required that the patient be told of this rare and remote risk. The appeals court disagreed:

60. In Katz, *Experimentation with Human Beings,* p. 534.
61. Ibid., pp. 536 and 534. Emphasis added.

We cannot agree that the matter of informed consent must be determined on the basis of medical testimony any more than that expert testimony of the standard of practice is determinative in any other case involving a fiduciary relationship. We agree with appellant that a physician's duty to disclose is not governed by the standard practice of the physicians' community, but it is a duty imposed by law which governs his conduct in the same manner as others in a similar fiduciary relationship. To hold otherwise would permit the medical profession to determine its own responsibilities to the patients in a matter of considerable public interest.[62]

Replacing the standard of the profession is the standard of the "reasonable man." In *Hunter* v. *Brown,* Judge James said: "Whether or not Dr. Brown violated his fiduciary duty in withholding the information is a question of fact to be judged by reasonable man standards."[63] Since 1969 there have been decisions in a number of states supporting these standards.[64]

The moral implication of these decisions is great. They affirm the right of the individual to information judged necessary by the reasonable man in spite of the possibility of a consensus among medical professionals that some part of the information may not be worth giving or may even be harmful. The policy implications are even greater. If the standard is now to be that of the reasonable person, with the explicit recognition that professional groups may incorporate biases systematically skewing their opinion about what is reasonable, then review mechanisms depending on the consensus of professional peers are no longer adequate.

Although the court cases have all involved consent for diagnostic procedures and treatment, not consent for experiments, they foreshadow increasing demands for lay representation and control mechanisms for reviewing research, insofar as the review deals with social and ethical issues.

In social policy research it is not clear what the relevant review group would be. It might include, but certainly would not be limited to, sociologists, psychologists, economists, and other scientists. It might also include federal bureaucrats and political appointees, state or local officials, and

62. *Berkey* v. *Anderson,* 1 Cal. App.3d 805, 82 Cal. Rptr. 67 (1969).

63. *Hunter* v. *Brown,* 484 P.2d 1162 (Wash. 1971).

64. *Dow* v. *Kaiser Foundation,* 90 Cal. Rptr. 747 (Cal. 1970); *Cooper* v. *Roberts,* 286 A.2d 647 (Pa. 1971); *Cobbs* v. *Grant,* 502 P.2d 1 (Cal. 1972); and *Wilkinson* v. *Vesey,* 295 A.2d 676 (R.I. 1972). For summary discussions of these developments see David S. Rubsamen, "Changes in 'Informed Consent,' " *Medical World News,* Feb. 9, 1973, pp. 66–67; and Joseph E. Simonaitis, "Recent Decisions on Informed Consent," *Journal of the American Medical Association,* vol. 221 (July 1972), pp. 441–42, and "More About Informed Consent, Part 1," ibid., vol. 224 (June 1973), pp. 1831–32.

community leaders. The elimination of standards of the profession and their replacement by the standard of the reasonable man would thus solve one problem, but might create another. How does one find the reasonable man and determine what levels of information he would find necessary for consent? The answer may be broadly based community review groups, as well as national social policy research review bodies, like the local and national lay review panels proposed for medical experimentation.

Additional Basic Elements of Consent

In addition to the elements of consent about which there is substantial consensus, several more controversial ones have been proposed.

THE PURPOSE OF THE RESEARCH. The HEW guidelines until 1974 did not specify that the purposes of the research be disclosed. Such disclosure is required in the principles of Nuremberg, the Declaration of Helsinki, and the 1954 World Medical Association Code, but strikingly not in the American Medical Association's principles. If the researcher and subject are viewed as a collegial team jointly pursuing knowledge for the benefit of the subject or society,[65] then the subject must have some knowledge of the purpose. But to disclose the purpose may jeopardize scientific validity. This conflict between scientific objectives and ethical requirements is not easily resolved. The withholding of information, however, poses a serious threat to the notion of informed consent.

One solution to the dilemma appears workable: In those rare, special cases where knowledge of the purpose would destroy the experiment (and only in those cases), it might be acceptable to ask a group of mock subjects drawn from the same experimental population if they would consent to participate in the experiment knowing its purpose. If there is substantial agreement (say, 95 percent), then it seems reasonable to conclude that most real subjects would have agreed to participate even if they had had the information that would destroy the experiment's validity.

THE PRESENCE OF A CONTROL GROUP. Knowing that a control or placebo is being used, some believe, could jeopardize research. The Food and Drug Administration's regulations require that subjects be informed of such a group, but other guidelines do not, although they generally re-

65. Talcott Parsons, "Research with Human Subjects and the 'Professional Complex,'" *Daedalus,* Spring 1969, pp. 325–60. Admittedly the notion of the collegial partnership is set forth as an ideal.

quire informing of risks.[66] Informing the subject that a control group is in the research design normally should not hurt the experiment. Of course, this would not require telling the subject whether he is receiving the placebo.

Social policy research may be quite a different matter. Subjects may be assigned to treatment groups before being contacted for enrollment. It is impossible to disguise the nature of the treatment as is normally done in medicine. Subjects in social policy research know in advance whether they are in the control or treatment group. In medicine it is the essence of the experiment to keep this information not only from the subject but from the researcher as well. I still find it objectionable for researchers to withhold the fact that different subjects will be getting different treatments. Systematically transmitting such information would eliminate some of the problems of accidental discovery. Certainly the community approving agency (such as the city council) would have to know of the different treatments. That information should not be withheld from the subjects.

NAMES OF REVIEW AND PATIENT PROTECTION AGENTS. Another basic element of any informed consent could be information about who has reviewed the experiment, and to whom the subject may turn for additional information or complaints about harmful effects.

STATEMENT OF BASIC RIGHTS OF THE SUBJECT. It is also advocated that subjects be protected by a Miranda rule requiring that they be informed of their basic rights. One such right—to withdraw from the experiment—is already included in the HEW guidelines. Giving a subject information about the treatment alternatives is not the same as telling him of a right to those alternatives. The developing right to health care might imply that, however. Several additional rights might be added to the list, including the right to care and to compensation for harmful consequences, the right to continued treatment should therapeutic research prove successful, and even the right to be an experimental subject.

RESPONSIBILITY FOR HARMFUL CONSEQUENCES. The subject should have the right to know who is responsible for harm done during research. One harmful side effect of the evolution of the informed consent doctrine has been the gradual withering of the recognized responsibility of the researcher for harm to the subject. Freund has observed that "two centuries ago it was said by a court of law that a physician experiments at his

---

66. The risk of a placebo group is unique. It is a risk of the distribution of effects.

peril."[67] In the nineteenth century the doctrine of researcher departing from standard medical practice at his own peril was the major protection of the patient against scientists eager for a place in history.[68] The peril of the researcher was, at least in part, that his reputation would suffer. Since the evolution of the consent doctrine, that peril has changed—in the folk beliefs of the experimenter if not in law—so that Freund might well say of the last half of the twentieth century that the physician experiments at the peril of the subject, the researcher being protected by the signed consent paper which he will hasten to produce in court. Even in cases of serious, costly, and morally inexcusable harm (such as the seven pregnancies that resulted from substituting placebos for birth control pills) virtually no attention has been given to compensation. Efforts of legal aid groups to provide counsel to the injured subjects have been met with the reply that the researcher is morally bound not to reveal the identity of the subjects.

Concern is rising over the right of the harmed subject to compensation for damages. Until recently one of the functions of the consent process has been to obtain written waiver of any claims for harm done. This waiving of legal rights is, however, prohibited in the HEW guidelines.[69] Yet even the guidelines do not state positively that some individual or agency is responsible for the harmful consequences and that the subject must be told who. Demands for clarification of this responsibility will grow. In insurance schemes being developed for harms arising unpredictably from experiments, the well-designed, properly reviewed, prudent risk-taking experiment to which the subject altruistically consented must be separated from unethical research conducted without proper review or reasonably informed consent.[70] No-fault insurance for subjects is needed. Neither the subject nor the competent, ethical researcher should have to bear the costs

67. Paul A. Freund, "Introduction to the Issue 'Ethical Aspects of Experimentation with Human Subjects,' " *Daedalus,* Spring 1969, p. viii.

68. See *Carpenter* v. *Blake* (1871) and *Jackson* v. *Burnham* (1895), cited in Katz, *Experimentation with Human Beings,* pp. 527–28.

69. "In addition, the agreement, written or oral, entered into by the subject, should include no exculpatory language through which the subject is made to waive, or to appear to waive, any of his legal rights, or to release the institution or its agents from liability for negligence." *Institutional Guide to DHEW Policy,* p. 7.

70. See Clark C. Havighurst, "Compensating Persons Injured in Human Experimentation," *Science,* July 10, 1970, pp. 153–57; and Irving Ladimer, "Clinical Research Insurance," *Journal of Chronic Diseases,* vol. 16 (December 1963), pp. 1229–35, and "Protecting Participants in Human Studies," *Annals of the New York Academy of Sciences, 1969,* vol. 169 (January 1970), pp. 564–72.

of unforeseen harmful consequences. However, by *no-fault* I mean that the harm must be demonstrated not to have occurred through fault of the researcher. It would be unfair for competent, ethical researchers to bear the burden of unethical or incompetent researchers' mistakes.

Responsibility for harm done in social policy research is a complicated problem. Most social policy research will probably have beneficial consequences for most of the subjects at least in the short run. Certainly harms will be pervasive, extremely difficult to define. There may well be psychological risks and long-term harms, but these will be nearly impossible to measure and prove. In a school voucher program a child may do worse in the school his parents choose than in the one he was assigned to; in a sterilization incentive test a participant may lose part of his family through death or divorce; in a housing experiment, readjustment problems may make a new neighborhood less attractive than the old. On both moral and practical grounds any individual or agency undertaking social policy research must face the question of responsibility for such possible consequences.

If social policy research differs from medical research in that harms, if they should occur at all, will be subtle, pervasive, and long term, then researchers must also face the question of the ethics of conducting such research.

The Right to Continued Treatment

Discontinuation of the experiment may be one harm expected to be particularly serious in social policy research. Therapeutic medical experimentation (the only kind with obvious risks in discontinuation) has normally been short term. The patient is either cured or killed. The literature on the ethics of medical experimentation is almost totally silent on the ethical obligation to continue useful treatment to a subject. Here medical ethics can learn from the discussion of the ethics of social policy research.

In social policy research, serious harm can come from stopping an experiment. In housing allowance programs the subjects may have abandoned their low-rent and possibly rent-controlled apartments; in health insurance tests, canceled their insurance; in educational experiments, destroyed the older school systems; in income maintenance experiments, committed themselves to installment payments or to a standard of living from which it would be psychologically difficult and possibly harmful to retreat. The cessation of such experiments will frequently raise ethical problems.

The attitude in medicine regarding continued obligation to research subjects is revealed in two classical studies of treatments for chronic illnesses in which the researcher was successful. In research on diabetes, insulin was demonstrated to be effective in dogs by Banting and Best in 1921.[71] By 1922, tests were conducted on humans by Banting, Best, MacLeod, Joslin, and others. I have searched for evidence that these researchers were concerned about their obligation to continue treatments of their patients; the issue simply is not addressed. Joslin in a later discussion of the early insulin cases summarized a follow-up study of the first eighty-three cases he treated in 1922 and 1923;[72] fifty-five of the patients had died (including two from diabetic coma). That a follow-up search was necessary suggests that the researchers did not maintain any continued sense of responsibility for those patients.

The insulin case is clouded, in that insulin became generally available soon after it was demonstrated effective in man. The development of cortisone treatment for arthritis is more revealing. One report describes research on twenty-three patients given cortisone and related compounds,[73] which at that time were scarce and very expensive. The researchers stressed continually that they considered their study on "clinical physiology" rather than clinical therapeutics, perhaps as a way of fending off criticism of their discontinuation of treatment. Their series of case reports describes dramatic improvements from cortisone followed by recurrence of symptoms when treatment was discontinued or a placebo was substituted. Case descriptions of follow-ups indicate that after the patients left the research, their conditions deteriorated. Apparently the research physicians thought they had no responsibility.

I have raised the question of obligation for continued treatment with a number of clinical pharmacologists working for drug companies or in hospitals. They all expressed concern for the subject's continued welfare, but in no case showed any evidence of having consciously thought about

71. F. G. Banting and C. H. Best, "The Internal Secretion of the Pancreas," *Journal of Laboratory and Clinical Medicine,* vol. 7 (February 1922), pp. 251–66.

72. Elliott P. Joslin and others, *The Treatment of Diabetes Mellitus,* 9th ed., rev. (Lea and Febiger, 1952), p. 267.

73. Philip S. Hench and others, "Effects of Cortisone Acetate and Pituitary ACTH on Rheumatoid Arthritis, Rheumatic Fever, and Certain Other Conditions," *Archives of Internal Medicine,* vol. 85 (April 1950), pp. 545–666.

the issue. None claimed to have developed or been taught a specific policy on continued responsibility.

In social policy research, as a minimum, a clear and carefully thought out policy must be developed prior to the initiation of research and made part of the informed consent. A minimum standard should be a guarantee of restoration at least to the subjects' former conditions or their equivalent.

There seems to be a difference in medical and social policy research in the extent to which researchers should be responsible for continuation and for harm done. While in medical research return of the patient to his former condition would be clearly unacceptable, in social policy research this is not unthinkable. Social policy research seems to treat subjects much as normal volunteers would be treated in medicine. In both cases there would seem to be a moral claim to restore the subject's prior condition to the extent possible. This must mean that social policy research subjects, while they are thought to be in need of intervention to improve their lot (as sick patients are), are not thought to be entitled to being maintained in the improved condition that the researchers temporarily place them in.

The Right to Be an Experimental Subject

Although there are limits on ethically acceptable research, strong moral imperatives push in the other direction as well. The case is stated forcefully (too forcefully) in Claude Bernard's claim that experiments that may do good are obligatory. The former director of the National Institutes of Health, Robert Marston, claims "there is immorality in *not* carrying out necessary research involving human subjects."[74]

It has been argued that the researcher has an obligation to society or to a patient to conduct research. Now, potential subjects are beginning to claim a right to have experimental treatment. The cases having the most merit are those where individuals with disabilities know of an experimental treatment and are not permitted access to it. Psychosurgery for the "criminally insane" is a major example. An individual with a history of violent behavior found not competent to stand trial is committed to a mental hospital for an indeterminate time. Medical examination may re-

---

74. "Medical Science, the Clinical Trial and Society," *Hastings Center Report*, vol. 3 (April 1973), pp. 1–4. See also Carl J. Wiggers, "Human Experimentation as Exemplified by the Career of Dr. William Beaumont," in Ladimer and Newman, *Clinical Investigation in Medicine*, p. 123.

veal abnormal brain physiology thought possibly treatable by surgical ablation (often by electrical coagulation). A recent research design proposed to provide psychosurgery for twelve patients and drug treatment for a like number. While release from confinement was not promised, participation in the experiment was seen by the first selected potential subject as his only or best chance of leading a relatively normal life free from periodic feelings of hostility and aggression. Yet the potential subject was barred from participation when the court argued that a mentally incompetent patient with the inducement of possible release can neither freely nor with rationality consent to the experimental procedure with potential harmful side effects described as "blunting of the personality" and "partial euthanasia."

It could be argued such a subject has a right to participate in experimental treatments. Or the subject could be argued to have a right to have his consent recognized as reasonably informed and voluntary, to be accepted by the administrators of the study in their appraisal of the proposed subject's welfare. They might refuse to include him in the experiment on other grounds such as the overwhelmingly high ratio of potential harm to benefit.

In social policy research the claim of the right to participate in experiments could be a serious problem. The high potential personal benefit from participation together with arguments of justice and fairness produce a strong case for inclusion. Since all people of the affected class cannot be included initially (or the research objective would be defeated), the selection principle must be based on some ethically defensible argument.

Publication of Unethical Research

The responsibility of publishers is a matter of continuing controversy. The British Medical Research Council has defended using ethical as well as scientific criteria for accepting material for publication. In their opinion, "it is desirable that editors and editorial boards, before accepting any communication, should not only satisfy themselves that the appropriate requirements have been fulfilled, but may properly insist that the reader is left in no doubt that such indeed is the case."[75]

A recent review of forty-three experiments that appeared to be ethically questionable on grounds other than consent revealed that in less than a

75. Memorandum MRC 53/649 (Oct. 16, 1953), cited in Katz, *Experimentation with Human Beings*, p. 936.

quarter was there any statement about the obtaining of consent. While one cannot conclude that it was not obtained, these were experiments that offered prima facie evidence that consent would be difficult to obtain. Beecher points out that researchers will have added incentive to be ethical if they are aware that publication depends on it.[76] Of course, the counter argument is apparent. Suppressing freedom to publish scientific findings is dangerous. Subjects have already undergone the risk. It is wasteful not to make use of the findings of the study. This is one of the controversial issues that will not be resolved soon, but those beginning to become involved in social policy research should be aware that controversy looms. Since social policy research will have diverse channels for publication, and in many cases will not find its end in publication at all, the control potentially exerted by publishers may not be as effective as it is in medical research.

In none of its aspects can the ethics of medical experimentation be transferred directly to the social policy field, but the newer research enterprises may learn from the experience of the older.

COMMENTS BY DAVID N. KERSHAW

Despite five years of social experimentation in the field, those directly concerned with the design and operation of experiments have done very little systematic thinking about ethical questions. This is not to say that ethical issues have been ignored; on the contrary, one of the most interesting aspects of the discussion of medical ethics is the organized framework it provides for putting together the disjointed pieces of ethical thinking in social experimentation. Indeed, virtually all of the principles discussed have, at one time or another, been carefully considered by social experimenters I have worked with in the operation of the New Jersey negative income tax experiment, the Seattle and Denver income maintenance experiments, the health insurance experiment, and the housing assistance supply experiment, and in the planning phase of the education vouchers experiment.

76. Henry Beecher, "Ethics and Clinical Research," *New England Journal of Medicine,* vol. 274 (June 1966), pp. 1354–60. Also see F. Peter Woodford, "Ethical Experimentation and the Editor," ibid., vol. 286 (April 1972), p. 892; and Maurice B. Strauss, "Ethics of Experimental Therapeutics," ibid., vol. 288 (May 1973), pp. 1183–84.

The practical experience of these five years ought to help in the development of a generally applicable set of ethical principles for social experimentation. As always, practical and operational considerations are bound to modify even the most carefully thought-out conceptual approach, and I will try to supply a modification of the principles suggested by Veatch that fits the social experiment case. These views cannot, however, be construed as representing those of social experimenters generally, for there has never been a consensus on ethical questions.

All of the experiments have a few general characteristics that bear directly on the way ethical principles are framed or on the way they can be applied and enforced in the field:

• The experiments are always large; that is, they contain a large number of subjects and a large number of staff members.

• Because of their complexity, experiments almost always involve more than one government agency, more than one level of government, and more than one operating organization.

• The experiments are often carried out at a number of sites, making communication difficult.

• The experiments always operate on extraordinarily tight time schedules requiring a relatively large number of snap decisions in the field.

• The people making those decisions are deeply engaged in the details of the undertaking and are not in a good position to develop and apply a thoughtful perspective to ethical problems.

• There is often a direct conflict between ethics and experimental efficacy which creates a considerable strain on social experimenters.

• Data from the experiments are stored in large computer data banks, and the problems of storage and processing often require the use of a number of computer facilities.

• Because they are visible within the community in which they operate, experiments are often subjected to political pressure or close public scrutiny.

• Because of their large budgets, and their potential impact on policy at the national level, experiments may be subjected to pressure and attempts at manipulation by the federal bureaucracy and the Congress.

• Because experiments deal with unexplored issues, it is virtually impossible to predict the kinds of problems and issues that will arise once the programs begin.

• Experiments almost always rely on subjects to supply verbally the data for analysis, which means that subjects' attitudes toward the research are critical; if one or more subjects believe that they are not being told the truth or that they are not being treated fairly, their noncooperative attitude can spread through the whole endeavor.

• Because individuals and families tend to cluster by social characteristics (income level, ethnicity, health status, condition of housing), subjects may often live very close to one another, even when they are assigned to different treatments.

In summary, these are not quiet, scientific studies undertaken in a carefully controlled laboratory context. They are large, noisy, fast moving, hectic, and usually public activities. This should be kept firmly in mind when applying the ethical experience from medical research. The characteristics of social experiments make the development and application of a set of ethical principles not only more difficult but, because of the large number of individuals simultaneously affected by a given decision in an experiment, in some ways even more compelling than the adoption of medical ethics has been.

Ratio of Benefit to Harm

The ratio of benefit to harm can be looked at from both a short-term and a long-term point of view. In the short term the benefit to the individual resulting from his participation should be measured against the harm to the individual resulting from his participation. In the long term the trade-off should be the harm to the individual resulting from his participation against the benefits to all individuals who might be eligible to participate in a new program introduced as a result of the experiment.

The experiments have a good record of carefully protecting subjects in the short term: the case in the income maintenance experiments is clear; in the health insurance experiment, subjects are at least as well off during and after as they were before the experiment; in the education vouchers experiment the case is less clear, although the subjects' increased individual choice without any offsetting loss is surely at least a short-term gain.

It is the long term that creates problems. Some participants in the income maintenance experiments might have lost their attachment to the labor force after three, four, or five years. Ineligibility for welfare or other sufficiently generous support programs could place them in dire straits. Some families in the housing experiment may find it difficult or impossible to find suitable housing after the experiment, or the experiment may have so inflated the general cost of housing as to strain all of the participants in the future. In the health insurance experiment, although considerable effort is made to insure that subjects keep a policy in force during the experiment, circumstances could arise in which subjects are uninsurable for a disease for which they would have been covered had the experiment not existed. In the education vouchers experiment, schools that cannot exist without the voucher funds may close when the support is withdrawn, leaving the community short of facilities.

It is possible that none of these harmful effects will result from the experiments. Indeed, experience suggests that they will not: few New Jersey families withdrew from the labor force and even those that did indicated no serious problems of readjustment after the experiment (although only the short-term effects are apparent now); in Seattle it appears that all families will be eligible for aid to families with dependent children if they so choose. It is, of course, too early to tell whether problems will arise with the other experiments. But the simple fact remains that if there are any long-term harmful effects, it is impossible to predict their kind and extent.

The long-term benefits from these research efforts come presumably in the form of better social programs for the class of people upon whom the research is conducted. The only information available on how experiments influence social policy is the brief experience with the family assistance plan proposed in the Ninety-first Congress. There was speculation that early New Jersey results had an impact on the decisions of the House Ways and Means Committee, although I do not think testimony on the negative income tax experiment was a central factor in the change in position of Representative Wilbur Mills. In the Senate Finance Committee the experiment was apparently automatically supported by supporters of family assistance and automatically attacked by its opponents. There was virtually no interest in the results of the experiment. Thus the one experience with long-term benefits is inconclusive. Of course the policy contribution of these efforts should not be to stimulate the introduction of new policy—most of which requires a basic set of social and political decisions inappropriate for experimenters to make—but to provide data that can be used either as a rational basis for choosing among new policy options or to define and modify new programs once the decision has been made to introduce them. In this regard it is even harder to predict (let alone measure and quantify) what benefits will accrue to those who participate in experiments: data from the experiments may be used to eliminate a program of benefit to the poor or to so modify a program that some participants are declared ineligible; in a host of ways the data could be used with unpredictable consequences for the participants.

I would not attempt to measure long-term benefits and harms in any systematic way because it is impossible to do so. Rather, I would provide a short-term protection that would require the experimenter to restore the status quo ante—to assure that, in the context of the passage of time and various exogenous events, subjects are left after the experiment as if it had never existed. This is a broad and complex principle, but it is more realistic and will result in more concrete protections for experimental subjects than an effort to predict all the potential costs and benefits of an experiment including those that are long term.

Voluntary and Informed Consent

The complex principle of consent has created many problems for field workers. They must decide not only what participants should be told but how much they must understand; they must also decide what can be offered to gain their consent and whether an institution may consent for them.

What are potential participants told?

The guidelines of the Department of Health, Education, and Welfare suggest six basic elements of information to be provided to subjects in social science research: an explanation of the procedures, a description of attendant discomforts and risks, a description of the benefits, disclosure of alternative procedures available, an offer to answer any inquiries, and an instruction that the subject is free to withdraw at any time.[77] In the experiments conducted to date, potential subjects have been told about their rights and obligations, assurances have been made about confidentiality of data within the limitations of existing law, the procedures to be followed for participation have been detailed, subjects have been assured that they may withdraw at any time, and they have been told that they may appeal any decision with which they disagree. This right of appeal goes slightly beyond the HEW guidelines.

77. *Institutional Guide to DHEW Policy*, p. 7.

Experience indicates that there may be risks that are completely un-anticipated and therefore cannot be described at the outset. In the New Jersey experiment, for example, some subjects had considerable trouble with local welfare departments as a direct result of their participation in the experiment. These problems could not have been predicted at the beginning of the experiment because they resulted from a law passed after enrollment. The television appearance of one New Jersey experiment subject, which he consented to by signing a release, triggered a completely unforeseen chain of events. The man was filmed at his place of work and was ridden by his foreman and fellow workers for being "somebody special" and for being called "poor" by the commentator; he lost the job after fighting with the foreman and could not find another; his wife left him, then filed for child support; he could not pay the child support and was threatened with imprisonment. The story ended happily when he found a new job and was able to pay child support. Could this have been anticipated? The fact that the environment in which these experiments operate cannot be controlled by the experimenter, that they are subject to public (and political) scrutiny, and that the time between enrollment and the end of the experiment is relatively long means that it is simply not possible to follow the medical experience of providing a comprehensive description of future risks. It seems to me that the ethical responsibility of the social experimenter is to describe those risks that he can reasonably foresee and to warn the participant that other unforeseen risks may arise. If the experiment is one in which a reasonable person, knowing what the experimenter knows, would enroll, then it is unnecessary for the experimenter to attempt to provide a catalogue of potential ill effects.[78]

78. Preston J. Burnham in a letter to *Science* suggests that hernia operation patients may encounter the following complications: "(1) Large artery may be cut and I may bleed to death. (2) Large vein may be cut and I may bleed to death. (3) Tube from testicle may be cut. I will then be sterile on that side. (4) Artery or veins to testicles may be cut—same result. (5) Opening around cord in muscles may be made too tight. (6) Clot may develop in these veins which will loosen when I get out of bed and hit my lungs, killing me. (7) Clot may develop in one or both legs which may cripple me, lead to loss of one or both legs, go to my lungs, or make my veins no good for life. (8) I may develop a horrible infection that may kill me. (9) The hernia may come back again after it has been operated on. (10) I may die from general anesthesia. (11) I may be paralyzed if spinal anesthesia is used. (12) If ether is used, it could explode inside me. (13) I may slip in hospital bathroom. (14) I may be run over going to the hospital. (15) The hospital may burn down." Quoted in Katz, *Experimentation with Human Beings*, p. 659.

How adequately do subjects have to understand what is told to them to be informed?

Peter Brown is concerned that subjects do not understand the experiments they participate in.[79] But it is not clear to me that from an ethical point of view subjects have to understand such things as the tax rate and guarantees they face. There are certain things that subjects should understand from a research point of view, and considerable discussion is under way about how much and what effect various levels of knowledge have on their response. Ethically, however, they should have to know what actions they should take to avoid being harmed by participation in the experiment. Even if their lack of knowledge causes them to take a course of action that leaves them relatively worse off (say, in terms of payments) than some other course of action, I do not think the resulting lower payment is unethical. From an ethical standpoint, subjects ought to be informed about when it is in their interest to drop out of the experiment; what will be done with the data they supply (so they can drop out or refuse to give answers if they disagree); when the experiment will end and what will be done to help them readjust; and the procedure to be followed if they wish to appeal a decision by the experimenters. If in the income maintenance case, for example, subjects have been adequately informed of the existence of alternative support programs, there should be no ethical issue raised if they feel they have received the wrong payment. If some other option for support in fact turns out to be more attractive, they know that they can switch from the experiment to that program.

While the record of educating subjects in the technical elements of their participation is at best mixed, those issues that are most appropriate from an ethical perspective are the ones families remember most easily. Harold Watts's contention that families "remember what they have to remember" has been pretty much borne out: almost all families enrolled in the experiments to date could give a rather precise termination date, knew they could drop out of the experiments (and did), and called the local office with questions about continuation of payments if they moved, the effect on the payments for new family members, and so forth. The most appropriate course seems to be to emphasize the important facts that will influence their decisions to participate, and to suggest strongly that they come to the local office for information if circumstances change. The

79. See p. 86, below.

provision of a copy of experimental regulations and occasional letters of reminder on critical points (welfare regulations, public housing eligibility, the date of termination) helps insure that they know what they should from the standpoint of experimental ethics.

When is consent involuntary?

The problem of excessive inducement, raised by both Veatch and Brown, creates special difficulties for the experimenter, particularly if the poor are considered to have few options and therefore no choices other than to remain destitute or to select the treatment proposed to them. As Veatch says, "voluntary consent will be extremely difficult to obtain," if it is meant to exclude "subtle forms of persuasion and psychological coercion."[80] It could be argued that a $3,000 per year income maintenance guarantee constitutes an incredibly large inducement to a poor family. But I would separate the program component of an experiment from the research component. In income maintenance, for example, the payments operation is the program component and the survey and analysis of survey data are the research component.

On the program side, two tests of ethical responsibility would apply: is the program one that a reasonable man, knowing what the experimenter knows, would agree to enroll in, and is the program one that would conceivably be adopted as national policy in the future? Even though the inclusion of extreme treatments might offer some analytic advantage, the experiments to date have never included a treatment that was not a relevant observation from the standpoint of policy. Using these criteria, the subject would merely be asked to participate in, or decline, a realistic program that could be available for him to participate in in the future.

It is on the research side that problems arise with inducements. One inducement is the payment usually offered to respondents for taking part in interviews. Generally, this payment has been within the guidelines proposed by Marston for research on prisoners ("reasonably related to the amounts paid for other services and not so high as to constitute undue inducement"[81]). When payments have exceeded their normal wage rate, subjects have often become suspicious. In several instances, however, when a great deal has been invested in a subject and one more interview with him is worth a great deal of money to the experimenter, Marston's

80. See pp. 33–34, above.
81. "Research on Minors, Prisoners and the Mentally Ill," p. 158.

rule has been broken. In both the New Jersey and the rural negative income tax experiments, special efforts were made toward subjects who had either moved away from the sample sites or who simply refused to take another interview. The purpose was to determine the characteristics of those who dropped out. Specially trained interviewers were authorized to offer generous inducements to subjects who were found; from a practical point of view, it did not make sense to run down the Jones family in Opolocka, Mississippi, and fail to get the interview for want of a marginal $50 worth of inducement. From an ethical point of view, this case would appear to be the inappropriate inducement that both Veatch and Brown caution against using to buy into the privacy of a family. However, an economist could argue (just as persuasively to me) that it is simply a case of meeting the respondents' price since there is a good economic reason for paying more. Since these respondents have refused before, they know there are no sanctions against their refusal and can feel free to consider the new offer.

Even if a respondent is always free to refuse an interview (or medical examination or housing inspection) and there are therefore no ethical strictures against raising the payment, just getting the data does not make it usable data. Field workers suspect that subjects who are reluctant to provide data give poor data.

A second inducement is the explicit threat to withdraw the treatment. In New Jersey, the program and research components were separated to the extent that refusal to participate in the interviews had no bearing on participation in the payments segment. In Seattle and Denver, however, subjects must continue to participate in the interviews in order to receive payments. This may constitute excessive inducement, particularly if the subject does not understand the number, length, and complexity of the interviews he must face once he is locked into the treatment.[82]

Experiments that clearly separate the program and research functions, with one test applied to the program side and another in the form of inducement compensation to the research side, appear to be in the clear ethically. Those that make submitting to the intrusions of the research side a condition of receiving the treatment are under a considerable obligation to explain the burdens of the research before the subject is asked to enroll.

82. While the experimenter should never create a situation where a respondent is locked in, the stimulus to resign rather than submit to one more interview may never be greater than the generous treatment. The average subject may not be able to identify the point at which an accumulation of marginal intrusions should tip the balance against participation.

Under what circumstances can institutions consent on behalf of their members?

Brown raises the issue of citizens of, say, Green Bay, being affected by the housing supply experiment without consenting individually to participate. The appropriate local political jurisdictions signed a memorandum of understanding consenting to the experiment. On the program side, the housing experiment is thus no different from any new program that affects the citizens of Green Bay; it is universal and was approved in advance by the duly elected representatives of the people. Indeed, new programs with a good deal more effect than this one are introduced with considerably less representation of the affected group. On the research side, individual consent is still required to induce subjects to submit to interviews and evaluations of the interiors of their homes.

Confidentiality

All of the experiments have paid a great deal of attention to confidentiality.[83] There appears to be general agreement that data collected from respondents (at least on interviews) should be kept strictly confidential. But there is no legal basis for protecting data, even where sophisticated and clever mechanical and physical ways of protecting information exist. I have been threatened with a contempt-of-court charge for refusing to turn over private information about subjects to a grand jury. Since there were no precedents in the social sciences and no laws, this created a difficult situation that was finally, and imperfectly, resolved by negotiation.

These are difficult times in which to argue for blanket protection of confidentiality. What is needed is a set of guidelines for social experimentation, perhaps like those already established for confidential communications: (1) the communications must originate in a confidence that they will not be disclosed; (2) the element of confidentiality must be essential to the full and satisfactory maintenance of the relation between the parties; (3) the relation must be one that in the opinion of the community ought to be sedulously fostered; and (4) the injury that would inure to the relation by the disclosure of the communications must be greater than the

83. See David N. Kershaw and Joseph C. Small, "Data Confidentiality and Privacy: Lessons from the New Jersey Negative Income Tax Experiment," *Public Policy*, vol. 20 (Spring 1972), pp. 257–80.

benefit that would be gained if the communications were admitted in litigation.[84] The social experiments conducted to date have conformed to these prerequisites for assignment to the confidential communication classification.

A confidentiality statute for social science research should be developed, to include the following elements:

(1) A definition of the subject matter to be covered, which should include personal, financial, social, and legal relationships. A satisfactory definition must make it possible to exclude frivolous and nonessential data from the protection of confidentiality.

(2) A stipulation that confidentiality will be granted only when the contract for the experiment is with a governmental agency, conducted for a governmental purpose, or conducted by the government. This stipulation would insure that the relationship is one the community wishes to foster.

(3) A provision that the original contract for the experiment and all agreements signed with participants specify that this act shall apply, in order to assure the confidential intent of the relationship.

(4) A provision defining certain exceptions—for example, the facts as to heinous crimes or very important evidence unobtainable elsewhere. This provision also must be tightly drawn if it is not to undermine all the protections of the statute. It should not allow a "fishing expedition" for evidence and probably should not come into force without court approval.

Without legal protection for the data provided, no blanket guarantee of protection can be given to subjects. In experiments thus far, they have been informed: "Data provided by you on this interview will be kept strictly confidential and will not be released without your written permission, *except as required by law*."[85] This rather ominous exception is difficult to explain, may frighten the subject, and clearly places pressure on field interviewers (who are interested in completing the interviews) to play down the qualification. This in turn runs solidly against the principle of informed consent.

Attempted intrusions into the New Jersey experiment by a grand jury, at least two welfare departments, the General Accounting Office, and the

---

84. Ibid., p. 274. See also John Henry Wigmore, *Evidence in Trials at Common Law*, rev. ed., vol. 8 (Little, Brown, 1961). For an excellent treatment of the problem with specific emphasis on the social sciences, see Paul Nejelski and Lindsey Miller Lerman, "A Researcher-Subject Testimonial Privilege: What to Do before the Subpoena Arrives," *Wisconsin Law Review*, vol. 1971, no. 4, pp. 1085–1148.

85. Emphasis added.

Senate Finance Committee suggest that this important issue should be attended to immediately.

The Right to Withdraw from Research

In the experiments conducted to date, all subjects have had the statutory right to withdraw, and the rules of operation have been explained to them. Approximately 25 percent of the enrollees in the New Jersey experiment and lower numbers in Seattle and Denver exercised this right. There is little doubt that families understand they are allowed to withdraw. But, as Veatch suggests, it may be impossible to withdraw because "the experiment itself may so change the social circumstances that former options are no longer open."[86] It seems to me that the problem of dropping out in the middle of the experiment is merely another form of the problem of ending the experiment: in either case the experimenter has the obligation of insuring the status quo ante. In income maintenance, for example, the researcher has the ethical obligation of insuring that participants are left in circumstances (presumably with regard to earning a living) identical to those they would have been in had the experiment never existed, no matter when they drop out; in the health experiment, to guarantee reinsurability at any time they drop out (which is being done by the simple means of keeping existing insurance in force); and so on. Once the ethical problems of terminating an experiment have been solved, it will be possible to deal with the ethical issue of subjects' real ability to make the choice to drop out.

The Adequacy of the Research Design

My criterion for deciding whether to field a social experiment requires a positive answer to four questions. The first is whether important data are missing that could prove decisive in the determination of a policy decision. Policymakers should answer this question before any design efforts begin, since only they can judge what is needed in order to make a policy decision. This is complicated, however, by the fact that those who decide to field an experiment are likely not to be in government to see its results. This is what makes it impossible to specify the benefit side of the ratio of benefit to harm.

86. Page 37, above.

The second question is whether all nonexperimental avenues for the research have been exhausted. The expense of field experiments makes it almost impossible to win approval for the technique unless the experimenter can demonstrate that all other methods of gathering the data have been exhausted.

The third question creates a real problem: has sufficient theoretical work been done to specify in advance a set of carefully designed hypotheses that can be tested? In the income maintenance experiments the economists had a solid theoretical basis for measuring labor-force response, and it was relatively easy to develop a direct, efficient, and tight set of income questions. Among the sociologists, however, there was a tendency to fish for relationships. The requirement that all data gathered had to be centrally related to the impact of a guaranteed income was no restraint at all on sociologists, since it could apply to an almost limitless list of items. Since the families had been selected and would be answering economic questions (which, according to my criteria, justified the experiment), why not collect other interesting information? Surely nobody could object to a few questions on fate control, anomie, happiness. The problem quickly became obvious: the first interview would have required about four hours. To date, the arguments for restricting length of questionnaires have usually revolved around the length of time subjects will be willing to be interviewed. There are no good rules about what should and should not be included on a questionnaire.[87]

The final question is whether the experiment can be expected to provide the needed data. If basic theoretical work is required before data are gathered, who is to judge one set of theories against another, particularly across disciplines? Basic research takes a great deal of time. Should field experiments with a high probability of providing useful information be held up until the theoretical work has been done?

Review of the Research

Whether peer review focuses on the subject or the experimenter, significant problems arise in applying this principle to social experiments.

87. One continuing check on experimenters is the Office of Management and Budget's right (under a 1951 executive order) to approve interview schedules, forms, and other means of communication and data gathering used in federally funded research projects. The procedure was designed to limit the burden on the population caused by useless, repetitious, or sensitive questions.

As Veatch points out, defining peers of the experimenter is difficult, since they come from a wide range of disciplines. Clearly some review takes place in the presentation of both research designs and results at meetings of professional societies, although it is often ex post facto. Given the underdevelopment of social experimental methodology, review sessions may fail to address the kinds of questions a medical review would cover, degenerating into professional bickering.

Social experiments are commonly reviewed by the institutions sponsoring them, although again the standard of review is not high. Either the institutional reviewers are no match for the experimenters in arguing technical points, or they have explicit nonresearch reasons for approving, rejecting, or modifying proposed research designs.

In several of the experiments, peers of the subject have been used in reviews, but in none successfully. In the New Jersey experiment the purpose and procedures of the experiment were explained to community representatives at several sites as a means of gaining their cooperation, and in several cases their cooperation made the survey possible. But this was not really a review, since it was not intended as a basis for making changes— indeed, any changes would have been disastrous from the research point of view. In Seattle the model cities agency was kept closely informed about the experiment, again mainly to gain their cooperation. The best example of subject peer review is Gary, where a local review board did have decision-making power over activities in the field. But the members of the review board did not understand the technical aspects of the research design and thus could not make informed judgments about important issues. Such critical items as varying treatments and random (or at least unbiased) assignment to treatments were never fully understood and arguments that delayed (and threatened) the research continued for some time.

One answer to the review problem would be to form a professional society of social experimenters. Although it clearly would be interdisciplinary, there is a set of common concerns that could form the basis of such a society. One of its first tasks would be the development of professional standards, including ethical principles. Since a society of social experimenters would include a wide spectrum of views, personal characteristics, and experiences, it might provide review committees with a combination of concerns that neither subjects, researchers, nor institutions could provide.

The Purpose of the Research

As Veatch points out, to disclose the purpose of the research may jeopardize the scientific validity of the results. That is certainly true in social science research since it is concerned with behavior of subjects as orally revealed. This behavior may be influenced not only by the pure treatment, but by such things as the subject's perception of the experimenter's expectations. To tell a subject in a health insurance experiment that you will be interested in how he utilizes medical services may well bias his response, particularly if the explanation is followed by frequent questions about his health.

We have never thought it necessary to go into details regarding the specific behaviors to be measured (knowing, of course, that to do so would risk the experiment). The important thing for the subject to know is what use will be made of the information he provides and what the range of possible policy outcomes will be. If he disapproves, he can refuse to contribute his information. In health research, therefore, the subject would be told that information provided by many individuals would be used by policymakers to make decisions about new or improved health delivery programs. I see no compelling reason for going into detail with subjects if all the ethical requirements can be met.

The Presence of a Control Group or Placebo

As I understand Veatch's point here, if an experiment includes a range of treatments, and subjects must agree to participate without knowing which of the treatments they will be assigned to, then all of the treatments must be explained to them. For example, if three pills of various strengths and a placebo are being tried out, the subjects must know the potential effects of each pill in addition to the fact that they may get a placebo.

If subjects were asked to participate in social experiments without knowing their treatment, Veatch's principle should be applied; that is merely a duplication of the informed consent principle whereby subjects should be aware of the costs and risks. However, in social experiments the subjects are assigned to the treatments before being contacted for enrollment. At that contact, the treatment to which they have been assigned is fully explained. Although they are not told of other treatments or of the control group, they are not subject to any of the other treatments and need not be told about them.

Strong evidence from the experiments contradicts Veatch's belief that informing the subject that there is a control group in the research design would not be detrimental to the experimental results. In all of the experiments conducted thus far, this would entail telling subjects at enrollment that there are other treatments, including a control group. But those assigned to a low treatment are likely to refuse to participate if they know that others are placed on a higher treatment. This is not just jealousy, but the feeling that they have been treated unjustly. Consider two Passaic families assigned to the New Jersey experiment according to the dictates of the research design. Family *A* consisted of four persons, had an income of $4,000 per year, and was assigned to a guarantee of $4,000 per year with a 50 percent tax rate. They thus could receive annual payments of $2,000 for a total annual income of $6,000. Family *B*, next-door neighbors and friends of Family *A*, had ten members, an annual income of $3,000 per year, and was assigned to a guarantee of $1,600 with a 50 percent tax rate, providing a total of $3,100 per year. The day after Family *A* was enrolled in the generous plan, an enroller came to the home of Family *B* with its less generous offer. Family *B* was enraged and refused to enroll in any program so clearly unjust. In similar circumstances, control group families have dropped out when learning of families who were receiving attractive treatments.

The nature of the social experiment process would seem to solve the conflict here, for subjects are randomly (or at least systematically) assigned to treatments before being asked to participate. Since they have no likelihood of being subjected to another treatment and thus no risk from it, no ethical responsibility is served by informing any subjects about other treatments.

Names of Review and Protection Agents

The income maintenance experiments have included an appeals panel to whom the subjects could turn if they disagreed with a decision by the experimenters. In New Jersey the panel was never used. Either subjects were not properly informed of its existence (although a detailed description of it was included in written information supplied to them), or they were afraid to use it. In Seattle, several subjects used the review board.

Statement of Basic Rights of the Subject

In the income maintenance experiments and in the health insurance experiment, detailed rules of operation are made available to all subjects. A short form of the rules in easy-to-understand language is provided before the decision to enroll, and all subjects sign an enrollment agreement, which is read word for word by the enroller. This agreement, in addition to getting the subject formally to recognize his obligations, explicitly states his rights. The health insurance enrollment agreement for the pilot group in Dayton includes the following terms:

I understand that by enrolling my family will receive the following benefits under the Plan:

A medical benefit plan with no premiums

Cash payments which may be spent in any way we choose

Assurance that no information obtained in the interviews by Urban Opinion Surveys which could be identified with any member of my family will be released without the written permission of the head(s) of the family, except if required by law.

I understand that by enrolling, I have the following obligations under the Plan:

To send a claim form to the Family Health Protection Plan whenever medical services are used

To submit a monthly summary of the medical care my family and I have received during the month

To participate in interviews conducted periodically by Urban Opinion Surveys

I also understand that my family has been urged to maintain health insurance or other medical coverage while participating in the Plan so that we will have coverage of our choice in effect when our participation in the Plan ends. If we do so, I understand that we will be reimbursed for our share of any premiums paid during the course of participation in the Plan to continue health insurance or other medical care coverage which we now have. I also understand that we will be reimbursed for our share of any premiums incurred, during the course of participation in the Plan, to obtain any other standard health insurance or medical coverage, although the Plan will not reimburse me for the costs of double or excessive coverage. While benefits under such other insurance must be assigned to the Plan while my family is participating, this should enable my family to have adequate coverage when our participation ends.

I further understand that the interviews which my family has taken or will take are directed toward gathering general information about our health. I understand that the interviewer is not a trained medical person and will not be able to evaluate the results of the interviews and we will not rely on him or his employer or others connected with this program to supply us with a medical diagnosis.

It has been explained to me that our continued participation in the Family Health Protection Plan is guaranteed, and may be terminated only upon ninety days prior notice because of complete or partial termination of government financing of the Plan or failure of my family to meet the obligations under the Plan. I understand that our participation and/or benefits otherwise payable under the Plan may be denied without notice in the event of fraud or mis-representation.

Finally, I understand that my family may withdraw from the Plan at any time.

Summary

After five years of practical experience, I strongly agree that a set of ethical principles is needed as guidance for social experimenters in the field. I agree with the principles that Veatch has proposed, though not always with the method or extent of his application of the principles to social experiments. Following his own conceptual framework, my set of principles would be:

• *Ratio of Benefit to Harm.* The notion of long-term benefit or harm should be eliminated since neither can be measured. The responsibility of the social experimenter is to assure the subject of the reinstatement of the status quo ante; that is, after the experiment is over, the subject should face a set of circumstances and opportunities that—in the context of the passage of time and other exogenous events—equal those he would have faced had the experiment never existed.

• *Informed Consent.* Experiments take place in an environment not entirely under the control of the experimenter. Therefore all risks cannot be specified in advance. The experimenter should not attempt to induce any subject to enroll in an experiment in which a reasonable man, knowing what the experimenter knows about the costs and the risks, would not enroll. In addition, the experimenter has an ethical responsibility to inform subjects of any changes in either experimental or environmental circumstances that he thinks may change risks to subjects (for example, the introduction of a new welfare law or public health program). Further, experiments should be thought of as consisting of a program segment and a research segment. The treatment, which makes up the program segment, should never be construed as an inducement, provided the experiment involves policy matters. Financial and other inducements to participate on the research side should in general follow the rule that subjects not be paid more than the rough equivalent of their opportunity wage; in special circumstances (for example, to gain one last interview with a subject who has repeatedly refused, and thus to help reduce the bias caused by no response) the experimenter should be able to raise the price offered for cooperation to the subject's price. This provides the subject with a clear economic choice, since he has the clear option of refusing again. The threat of withdrawal of the treatment for failure to conform to research requests represents an excessive inducement to subjects to remain in an experiment; experimenters have a special responsibility to inform subjects of the costs and risks of the research in advance of enrolling them. Finally, saturation experiments are not unethical provided that they have the consent of the duly elected officials of the jurisdiction in which the experiment will operate. The program segment of such experiments is no different from any new program and the research segment is still subject to individual voluntary consent.

• *Confidentiality.* Real threats have been made against subjects and researchers because of the lack of a legal basis for protecting privileged communications. A confidentiality law is needed that carefully defines the subject matter to be covered, the sponsors who are eligible to have research covered, and the exceptions that will assure that the community good is not violated by the protection of important evidence that is unobtainable elsewhere. The absence of such a law makes the operation of experiments very difficult, despite increasing sophistication with physical and mechanical means of protecting data.

• *Right to Withdraw.* All experiments have provided the statutory right to withdraw, and a relatively large number of families have chosen to do so. The experimenter's responsibility to assure the status quo ante when the experiment ends should apply also to the end of any subject's participation. The subtle problem of whether subjects can really withdraw can thus be dealt with in terms of the ratio of short-term benefits to harms.

• *Research Design.* No experiment with human subjects should take place unless important data that would influence policy are needed, all nonexperimental avenues have been exhausted, sufficient theoretical work has taken place prior to the experiment to allow the testing of carefully formulated hypotheses, and it has been determined that a social experiment, with all its limitations, will in fact yield the data wanted. The greatest ethical danger is not from the fielding of unnecessary experiments but the collection of unnecessary data—and the increased intrusion on subjects—once an experiment has begun. No solution is suggested for this problem.

• *Review of Research.* Institutional, subject-peer, and researcher-peer review mechanisms have proven inadequate in social experiments. Thought should be given to the formation of a professional society of social experimenters from which peer reviews (and such other things as ethical standards) could emanate.

• *Explanation of Purpose.* There should be no ethical responsibility to inform subjects in analytical detail about the intent of the research, provided they are fully informed of what use will be made of the information they provide and what the range of possible policy outcomes based on the information will be. To require income maintenance researchers to explain to respondents that they are measuring hours worked and changes in wage rates is unnecessarily precise and can threaten the research.

• *Control Groups.* To ask a subject to enroll in advance of the assignment of treatments requires that he be fully informed about all treatments, including the control group, to which he could be assigned. In experiments where an irreversible decision is made on assignment before the subjects are approached, there is no ethical responsibility to describe other treatments to a subject, provided he understands his own. Informing subjects has endangered some social experiments.

• *Appeals Panels.* Experiments to date have always included appeals panels to whom subjects could turn to dispute a decision. The fact that few subjects have used the panels probably means that subjects have not been effectively informed of their existence.

• *Subjects' Rights.* Experiments to date have always included an enrollment agreement which subjects signed and which indicated both rights and responsibilities. Detailed copies of the experiment regulations are maintained and are available to subjects, and a short form of the regulations, written in easy-to-understand language, is presented to the subject before the decision to enroll is made.

PETER G. BROWN

Informed Consent in Social Experimentation: Some Cautionary Notes

This paper seeks to evaluate the use of informed consent to protect the rights and welfare of individuals affected by large-scale social experiments. It suggests that in some circumstances the doctrine of informed consent must be applied with caution.[1] For this discussion, a social experiment is defined as an intentional intervention in an economic or social system designed to yield results useful in the formulation of public policy, where this intervention involves a sample of the human population and sometimes a control group.[2] Medical and psychological experiments with human subjects are not considered, though many of the problems of social experimentation afflict them as well.

Most of the federally funded social experiments currently under way, or contemplated, draw their samples mainly from lower-middle-income or low-income persons because the policies under study are aimed at persons

1. Alternatively, the evaluation of ethical issues involved in experimentation could be based on the overall costs and benefits to be derived from it. It might be argued that ethical issues could be handled in this context because these calculations would include the effects of the experiment on the welfare of those affected by it, and estimates of the increased welfare to be gained by others due to improved policies, and the costs of these new policies. But this approach glosses over the question of what kinds of costs are permissible in return for what kinds of benefits. Would cost-benefit analysis permit substantial harms to some individuals for moderate gains to millions? Are there circumstances under which these costs may not be imposed? Answers to questions of this kind must precede imposition of cost-benefit techniques. The informed-consent framework is designed to lay out plausible sets of rules on which agreement is possible (or at least where disagreement may be clearly focused) so that the techniques of cost-benefit analysis may be applied.

2. Some of the experiments discussed lack control groups as such and compare the sample to similar elements of the population at large.

79

in these groups. Though the experimental process need not be limited to these classes, this discussion concentrates on the implications of social experimentation for these groups.

In two areas, informed consent must be used very carefully for handling ethical issues in social experimentation. First, it may be that the ability of individuals to consent truly and freely will vary. This will prove particularly troublesome morally in experiments that involve risk or invasion of privacy. Similarly, the consent doctrine may in some circumstances dictate a method of drawing the sample that is opposed to what would be preferable from research and policy points of view. Second, where parents are asked to consent for their children there are limits on their legitimate powers to do so. Caution is also required in a third, related area: in experimental situations involving substantial effects on nonparticipants their "tacit" consent should not be *presumed*.

The Doctrine of Informed Consent

Informed consent is the principal standard for protecting individuals set forth in *The Institutional Guide to DHEW Policy on Protection of Human Subjects*.[3] To insure that experiments adhere to the HEW standards, institutions governed by the guidelines are required to establish committees to review the procedures and the risks to subjects in any experiments they conduct. The income maintenance, housing allowance, and health insurance experiments follow this basic doctrine of informed consent.

Meaning of "Informed" and "Consent"

A person can be said to be informed when he has been given and has understood all aspects of the experimental situation relevant to his own rights and well-being or those of his children or any other person for whom he is responsible.[4]

3. Issued by the U.S. Department of Health, Education, and Welfare, DHEW Publication (NIH) 72-102 (Dec. 1, 1971). Rules set forth in the guidelines are outlined on pp. 23 and 31–32, above.

4. For a thorough discussion of the barriers to fully informed consent, see Jay Katz, with the assistance of Alexander Morgan Capron and Eleanor Swift Glass, *Experimentation with Human Beings* (New York: Russell Sage Foundation, 1972), pp. 609–73.

Though many aspects of the experimental procedure need not be revealed to the subject, who decides what is to be revealed, and what is not, is an important issue. Assuming the proper procedural safeguards are being followed, the way the data are manipulated for statistical purposes is irrelevant, though the characteristics of the safeguards are not. The overall policy purpose of the experiment is relevant because the person may not wish to contribute to the formulation of policies he considers pernicious. Wolfensberger correctly proposes in general that

consent be considered "informed" when all essential aspects are understood by the subject. Essential aspects consist primarily of information regarding the "rights" . . . yielded to an experimenter by a subject; the types and degrees of risk involved; and the detrimental or beneficial consequences, if any, that may directly affect the subject. Explanation of the purpose of a study should probably be considered a desirable but not essential element unless the results could affect the subject directly. Some experiments are so technical as to be unintelligible even to scientific peers from outside a specialty area; they could not be meaningfully explained to many or any lay subjects. It is particularly important that the potentially endless detailing of minutiae of an experiment, per se, does not come to be considered the only adequate method of informing.[5]

Whether the subject understands what he has been told is a more troublesome question. The only way of being sure that a subject in an experiment comprehends the rules he must observe in order to remain in an experimental group is to have him apply them. Then it is possible to observe whether he can repeat the information in a nonrote fashion, how he behaves during the course of the experiment, directions he gives to others, and so on. For these reasons, consent forms that ask a person to restate in writing what he has agreed to seem desirable. In many circumstances it would seem desirable to test individuals rather early in an experiment to determine whether they understand what they have agreed to.

Consent is an even more complex notion, including at least these elements: it creates a right or set of rights; it is based on a particular though widely shared model of human decision-making; and it implies a "signal" of agreement; moreover, informed consent involves freely consenting.

Consent can be regarded as an "expression of a wish by one man [the subject] that another man [the experimenter] should act in a certain way, known and intended to create or increase in the latter the right to act in

5. Wolf Wolfensberger, "Ethical Issues in Research with Human Subjects," *Science,* January 6, 1967, pp. 48–49.

this way."[6] A person who consents to participation in an experiment, for instance, creates rights for the institutions and persons conducting the experiment that they would not otherwise have.[7] They are given rights to gather information, to observe, to affect participants in certain ways.

Both the theory of consent (in classical and contemporary political philosophy) and ordinary usage of the word *consent* suppose that the persons consenting are in some sense rational beings.[8] Inherent in this concept of *rational being* is the idea that humans are not only capable of planning, but have at least loosely constructed life objectives.

Even to so pessimistic a commentator on human nature and behavior as Thomas Hobbes it appears that a measured calculus will cause men to civilize their natural passions and adopt a political society to insure their long-term well-being. Hobbes argues that consent to government is based on reasoned estimates about how to arrange the future. Moreover, in consenting to the creation of the state, men consent to something that is coterminous with the interests they are trying to protect: "Nor is it enough for the security which men desire should last all the time of their life that they be governed and directed by one judgment for a limited time, as in one battle or one war."[9] Hobbes is not implying that consent cannot be withdrawn if one of the parties fails to live up to the agreement, but that consent depends on a rational plan that covers at least the period of time that the agreement is expected to be in force. For example, according to Hobbes, men will need protection from other men for the full course of their lives.

The concept of a personal life plan implies the subordinating of some objectives and ends to others.[10] Each person has a set of objectives to which he will allocate the resources given to him under the circumstances.

---

6. J. P. Plamenatz, *Consent, Freedom and Political Obligation*, 2nd ed. (London: Oxford University Press, 1968), p. 18. Plamenatz is mainly concerned with explicating the concept of "consent of the governed."

7. Consent as a right-creating action is different from approval (see ibid., pp. 15–19). A person may approve of all sorts of actions on the part of others that he cannot consent to, in part because the rights on which the actions are based are not his to create.

8. John Rawls's theory of consent is based on what rational men would choose; unfortunately, he does not fully explain his concept of rationality. See *A Theory of Justice* (Harvard University Press, 1971), p. 142.

9. Thomas Hobbes, *The Leviathan* (Bobbs Merrill, 1958), p. 141.

10. See Charles Fried, *An Anatomy of Values: Problems of Personal and Social Choice* (Harvard University Press, 1970), pp. 97–101 and 155–77.

Anyone who lacks such objectives (at least for the period of the experiment) cannot be said to consent.

Consent also implies a signaling or sign of some kind. The consenter is asked to sign a contract, nod, say "okay" to give notice that he has understood and agreed.

Moreover, informed consent, as used in the context of experiments, means free and informed consent. Although consent may carry with it the notion of freedom, some choices can be coerced—for example, a person may be informed about an experiment and have agreed to it, but he could have consented under coercion.

The relative attractiveness of an offer changes under various circumstances, and the more attractive an offer, the less able is a person to resist it. When an offer is very attractive, the experimenter must be especially certain that the subject is fully informed about the experiment and understands what he is being asked to agree to. One way to avoid the difficult problem of assessing a person's ability to consent, though not universally useful, is to rule out very attractive offers. This is probably the reason the HEW guidelines state that "compensation to volunteers should never be such as to constitute an undue inducement."[11]

Reasons for the Doctrine

The idea that the moral issues involved in social experimentation can be resolved by securing the consent of those affected is based in part on the notion that persons should be free to determine their own behavior because freedom is a good in itself. Holders of this natural law view might assert, as did John Locke, that being free is a natural right.[12] Such freedom belongs to a person prior to any set of conventions or agreements, and is taken by contract theorists, such as Locke, to be the source of legitimacy for those conventions and agreements. Since freedom is the primary value, it can be restricted only by itself, and the restrictions must be carefully

11. *Institutional Guide to DHEW Policy,* p. 7.

12. "To understand political power aright, and derive it from its original, we must consider what state all men are naturally in, and that is a state of perfect freedom to order their actions and dispose of their possessions and persons as they think fit, within the bounds of the law of nature, without asking leave, or depending upon the will of any other man." John Locke, "An Essay Concerning the True Original, Extent, and End of Civil Government," in Edwin A. Burtt, ed., *The English Philosophers from Bacon to Mill* (Random House, 1939), p. 404.

justified. Hence, it is a feature of contract theory that restrictions on freedom must be agreed to.[13] When persons involved in experiments risk a limitation of their freedom and a change in their circumstances, they are asked to consent to this limitation of this good.

A second argument for consent is based on the idea that each mature individual is best able to promote his own well-being. In this sense, characteristic of utilitarians, freedom is seen as an instrumental value. Mill's argument for individual freedom could well be used as a basis for securing the consent of those affected:

Neither one person, nor any number of persons, is warranted in saying to another human creature of ripe years, that he shall not do with his life for his own benefit what he chooses to do with it. He is the person most interested in his own well-being: the interest which any other person, except in cases of strong personal attachment, can have in it, is trifling, compared with that which he himself has; the interest which society has in him individually (except as to his conduct to others) is fractional, and altogether indirect; while with respect to his own feelings and circumstances, the most ordinary man or woman has means of knowledge immeasurably surpassing those that can be possessed by anyone else. The interference of society to overrule his judgment and purposes in what only regards himself must be grounded on general presumptions; which may be altogether wrong, and even if right, are as likely as not to be misapplied to individual cases, by persons no better acquainted with the circumstances of such cases than those are who look at them merely from without. In this department, therefore, of human affairs, individuality has its proper field of action.[14]

Consent, then, operates both to protect basic rights such as freedom, and to make it possible for people to maximize their own welfare.[15]

Relying on Informed Consent

The reliability of informed consent in protecting the rights of subjects varies, depending on how rational, informed, and self-interested the consenter is, and how successful the experimental treatment is in improving the condition and avoiding risks or invasion of privacy of the subject.

13. See Rawls, *A Theory of Justice*, pp. 136–50.

14. John Stuart Mill, "On Liberty," in Burtt, *The English Philosophers*, pp. 1008–09.

15. Hence it can be argued in experimental situations that individuals consent because they believe ex ante that participation will be beneficial to them. This does not mitigate the responsibility of the experimenter to maximize the chance that this judgment will be correct, nor his responsibility to insure that they are truly able to consent.

These two factors must be considered simultaneously. "The reason we balk at a man selling himself into slavery is not simply that *this* consent precludes *future* consent, but also because of the sort of relationship slavery is."[16] The more a subject is placed at risk or his privacy is threatened, the more necessary is it to assure that he can truly consent.

In experiments involving populations of adults, the reliability of informed consent varies with the extent to which the subjects possess information needed for rational deliberation, and with the extent to which they are placed at risk or their privacy threatened. These conditions may be represented by two axes:

$$\longleftarrow \hspace{8cm} \longrightarrow$$

Full information   *Poor information or none*
(full capability for rational deliberation)   *(impaired deliberative capability)*

$$\longleftarrow \hspace{8cm} \longrightarrow$$

No risk   *Substantial risk*
(complete privacy)   *(privacy impaired or threatened)*

Barriers to autonomy and rational decision making, failures of communication and comprehension, and so on, affect the ability to consent,[17] represented by the upper axis. These barriers are not immobile, however, and the location of an individual on this axis can be changed through education or careful presentation of information. Similarly, risk, represented by the lower axis, can be reduced through changes in experimental design and in the assignment of individuals to various cells in that design.

The more an experiment involves risks and the less individuals are able to freely give their informed consent, the less the concerns expressed in the consent doctrine can be satisfied. An experiment that connects the left ends of the two axes is optimal from a moral point of view.[18] An experiment that connects the right ends of the axes is morally unacceptable, except under very unusual circumstances. When the right end of one axis is connected with the left end of the other, care is required in executing the experiment, but there is no prima facie case against going ahead with it. Intermediate cases present problems of varying severity.

These points may be illustrated by reference to some actual experiments.

16. J. Peter Euben, "Walzer's Obligations," *Philosophy and Public Affairs,* vol. 1 (Summer 1972), p. 446.

17. Katz, *Experimentation with Human Beings,* pp. 609–73, fully enumerates these factors.

18. In cases where the invasion of privacy and risk are fully zero, consent may not be required. Some data collection efforts are like this, though they are probably more usefully thought of as observations than as experiments. None of the experiments considered in this paper fits this model.

Where Informed Consent Is Most Appropriate

The New Jersey income maintenance experiment is aimed primarily at determining the effect of cash grants of varying amounts on the incentives, of low-income families to work. It appears that most recipients have used the increased income to improve their family welfare. For these individuals there is not only a monetary gain from participating in the experiment, but there may be a substantial lifetime and life-style improvement.

If the persons in the experiment are rational and able to defend their own interests and if conditions of termination were clearly explained, and understood, there seems to be little of which to complain. In a context such as this, it appears that the consent doctrine is both necessary and sufficient.

Unfortunately, there is some indirect evidence that participants in an experiment such as this may not understand how many of the rules would affect their income, how long they would be eligible for payments, and how participation was affected by other choices they might make, such as moving.[19] This raises difficult questions about the effectiveness of informed consent in complicated social policy experiments (especially since the income maintenance experiment is probably easier to comprehend than most others). Many individuals may agree to a system of rules and conditions of termination that they do not understand, and through their own miscalculation may suffer substantial harm from participation in an experiment.

Where Consent Doctrine Is Less Appropriate

Because experiments can make persons worse off in a variety of ways, it is useful to identify the kinds of risks they pose. *Direct risks or harms,*

19. In a survey to test how well the 1,108 families in HEW's Seattle income maintenance experiment understood the rules of the experiment, responses were received from 77 percent of the participants. There was a statistically significant difference between the number of correct answers given by black families and by white families, and by one- and two-parent families. Correct responses by black one-parent families, black two-parent families, white one-parent families, and white two-parent families were: 48 percent, 65 percent, 68 percent, and 80 percent on how fulltime work affected their grant; 48 percent, 47 percent, 68 percent, and 72 percent on how quitting a job would affect their payments; 6 percent, 13 percent, 31 percent, and 37 percent on how large a family income would reduce their payments to zero; and 58 percent, 62 percent, 73 percent, and 78 percent on how much longer the family would be eligible to receive income maintenance payments. Stanford Research Institute, memorandum (1972).

such as a reduction in income or insurance benefits, are those caused by the experiment itself. *Induced risks or harms* are those brought on by other persons or institutions that harm the experimental subject—the health insurance experiment, for instance, might cause doctors to provide less care to their patients. *Risks or harms of termination or phaseout* result from the removal or reduction of the beneficial treatment. *Community risks or harms* are those that affect persons not in the sample or control group of the experiment itself; any experiment that increases the competition for a desired commodity can have this sort of effect.

Still another type of harm or risk can arise from *goal conflict*. The performance contracting experiment of the Office of Economic Opportunity was designed to test the idea that the reading and mathematical ability of children might be improved by paying private contractors to educate children, and making payment contingent on the educational performance of the children. From the point of view of the parents, their children could be harmed by being assigned to contractors whose educational philosophy differed from theirs—a parent enamored of Montessori methods would be aghast to have his child assigned to a Skinnerian contractor.[20] The performance contracting experiment also posed *unpredictable risks* because it was not based on a theory of education, but on a general (difficult to falsify) hypothesis about utility-maximizing behavior of contractors.[21] The types of risks attendant to such experiments may be difficult to specify because the behavioral changes they induce are unpredictable. For this reason experiments that test vague hypotheses should be avoided as a rule.

Not only can risks or harms be of different kinds, but they can be of many forms: loss of money, health, emotional stability, friends; destruction of a family; loss of a well-known neighborhood and the like.

Two of the current social experiments pose the possibility of two of these types of risks.

INDUCED RISKS OR HARM. In the health insurance experiment, persons are assigned to insurance plans with varying combinations of coinsurance and deductible costs. Participants must discontinue their present coverage

20. Apparently some parents were not given the opportunity to consent on behalf of their children. See Education Turnkey Systems, *Final Report to the Office of Economic Opportunity: Performance Incentive Remedial Education Experiment* (Washington: Education Turnkey Systems, 1971), p. 198. This is clearly outrageous.

21. I am indebted to Michael Timpane for this point. Perhaps such risks could be avoided, or at least revealed, by imagining the circumstances under which the experimental hypothesis could be falsified. Those hypotheses that satisfy too many conditions may be suspect from this point of view.

and take on coverage assigned them by the experiment which, in some cases, may not be as comprehensive as their former policies. Steps have been taken, however, to keep participants from being made worse off financially.

For both ethical and experimental reasons, it is desirable that families not be made worse off from participating in the experiment. The experimental reason is that we wish random refusals to participate and random attrition by type of plan. If families who *ex post* had substantial medical expenditures could be worse off in certain plans but not in others, families who *ex ante* expected to have substantial medical expenditures would tend to refuse plans differentially. This would tend to bias the estimated elasticity.[22]

To overcome this problem, the experimenters state that families will be compensated in cash for any financial losses flowing from participation. These families can dispose of the money when and as they choose.

In spite of these provisions, the experiment contains two examples of possible induced risks or harms. The experiment is designed to

collect information on the types of health services that are most used under the various insurance plans. The standard insurance coverage with emphasis on in-patient services is believed to result in the over use of hospital facilities. The experiment will test several variations on the type of service covered. For example, it will be possible to cover all costs of visits to a doctor's office while having the patient share hospital costs. This should result in greater use of out-patient care than under standard insurance coverage. The implication of this for health status and costs can be examined by making comparisons with plans in which patients share in costs of all services and other plans in which all services are free. Variations of this sort will provide information that can contribute greatly to the planning necessary to make any innovative public or private health care system work.[23]

Obviously, this particular treatment is designed to decrease hospital utilization. Further, it contemplates testing how these changes in utilization affect health. It is at least possible that persons who should be hospitalized will be treated on an outpatient basis. Some of the persons in the sample will be poor and, despite precautions, unable to cover the portion of hospital bills not taken care of under the insurance scheme. This creates an incentive for both the individual and the physician to avoid hospital care. Moreover, many poor persons have no personal physician who has a continuing interest in their welfare. As a consequence, the interest of

22. Joseph Newhouse, *A Design for a Health Insurance Experiment* (Santa Monica: Rand Corp., 1972), p. 32.

23. U.S. Office of Economic Opportunity, Office of Planning, Research, and Evaluation, Policy Research Division, "The Health Insurance Experiment: Descriptive Summary" (n.d.; processed), pp. 4–5.

the doctor in the welfare of his patient, a cornerstone of medical ethics, may be weak or nonexistent. These circumstances conspire to create a situation where a participant in the experiment runs some risk of harm. One possible consequence, however remote, is death.[24]

The same kind of risk applies to individuals whose experimental treatments involve high deductible costs for outpatient care (some are as high as $400).[25] Those whose deductible costs for both inpatient and outpatient care are high ($400 for each type of deduction for each person[26]) are, in a sense, doubly exposed to hazards of this sort. The poorer the person, despite cash payments for participation, the stronger the incentive not to utilize medical care.

RISKS OF TERMINATION. The housing allowance experiment, which is designed to look at how families change their demand for housing services when offered cash grants, illustrates some of the risks associated with termination of an experiment. Some of the families receive grants with no strings attached, while others must live in housing approved by those running the experiment in order to continue receiving their grants. Persons in the second category are particularly vulnerable to harm at the termination of the experiment. Many of them will have had to move to housing that meets the experimental standards (of course, some may negotiate with their landlord to improve the quality of their present housing so that it will meet the standards), and the new housing may cost considerably more than their old housing.

Suppose a family moves into the higher quality, higher cost housing and enjoys the benefits of this relocation for the length of the experiment. At the end of the experiment the extra cash is withdrawn and the family must find other housing. The housing they formerly occupied will probably be occupied by someone else, or abandoned, by the time they return to the housing market. In addition, if they had not participated in the ex-

---

24. The conclusion that imposing certain risks on others (as when people don't truly consent to an experiment of this sort) is prima facie immoral can be reached by beginning with the question: when may we impose grave risks on others? If man is conceived of as a rational being, and a being who has a life plan, these risks are ruled out and cannot be imposed except under unusual circumstances. "While the grave risks I would take for myself will be tied specifically to a crucial end, the grave risks imposed on me would be random over my life cycle." (Fried, *An Anatomy of Values*, p. 192. Obviously, specifying what constitutes a grave risk will be a problem.) Imposing risks on others who cannot or do not consent violates the very concept of moral behavior, except under extraordinary circumstances (see pp. 92–99, below).

25. See Newhouse, *Design for a Health Insurance Experiment*, p. 24.

26. Ibid.

periment and had remained in their old dwelling, their rents might not have risen as high as the rents they now must pay on returning to the market.[27] As a consequence, it may be impossible for them to obtain housing of the same quality they occupied prior to the experiment, so that ultimately they will be worse off for having participated.

If the participants are rational persons who freely consented (on the basis of adequate information) to be in the experiment, it can be argued that they have no one to blame but themselves. They agreed to accept the benefits of better housing and did enjoy this benefit and had to weigh this against other options open to them. So, while they may have been made worse off, it is a rational choice in which they have participated. A problem arises only if the individuals were not truly able to consent to the procedure in question.

In the present design for the experiment, steps have been taken to minimize these problems.

Nine months prior to start of scheduled phaseout operations, SRI and HUD, with selected specialists, shall have developed a plan and instruments necessary to assure that participants in the program can remain, wherever possible, in the residences they occupy at the time of phaseout and receive continuing federal assistance. Households unable to qualify to remain in their homes will be guaranteed assistance from a similar housing program for which they are eligible or will have their approved moving expenses paid by SRI to housing which the household can afford.[28]

Though individuals will have help in finding other housing, there is no guarantee that the housing (even when public) will be of the same quality as the housing from which they moved.

The Principle of Inverse Selection

The more there is reason to believe that a person is exposed to risk, the more the experimenter should rely on what can be called the "principle of inverse selection."[29] In writing about medical experiments, Jonas argues that from a moral point of view the best subject is "the physician-researcher himself and the scientific confraternity at large."

27. See Raymond J. Struyk, assisted by Sue A. Marshall, "Estimating the Value of Housing Services with Census Users' Sample: Comparative Results for Five Areas," working paper 208-10 (Washington: Urban Institute, 1973; processed), for evidence that those who move more frequently tend to pay higher rents.

28. Stanford Research Institute, *Design Document, Housing Allowance Experiment Program* (Palo Alto: SRI, 1972), p. 804.

29. See Hans Jonas, "Philosophical Reflections on Experimenting with Human Subjects"; reprinted in Katz, *Experimentation with Human Beings*, pp. 667–69.

If the properties we adduced as the particular qualifications of the members of the scientific fraternity itself are taken as general criteria of selection, then one should look for additional subjects where a maximum of identification, understanding, and spontaneity can be expected—that is, among the most highly motivated, the most highly educated, and the least "captive" members of the community. From this naturally scarce resource, a descending order of permissibility leads to greater abundance and ease of supply, whose use should become proportionately more hesitant as the exculpating criteria are relaxed. An inversion of normal "market" behavior is demanded here—namely, to accept the lowest quotation last (and excused only by the greatest pressure of need), to pay the highest price first. . . .

Let us note that this is the opposite of a social utility standard, the reverse of the order by "availability and expendability": The most valuable and scarcest, the least expendable elements of the social organism, are to be the first candidates for risk and sacrifice.[30]

The experimenter seeks to sample the target population, or at least some sections of it, randomly; but the ability to truly consent will vary among individuals, probably along a continuum.[31] Barriers to consenting include lack of practice in making decisions, lack of education, information inaccurately conveyed or difficult to understand, the power roles between experimenter and subject being played out in the context of the consent decision, difficulty in articulating lifetime objectives, and difficulty in rationing between present and future consumption.[32] The principle of inverse selection serves as a heuristic device to remind the experimenter of the characteristics of persons most able to consent. To fully satisfy the concerns underlying informed consent, the more risk is involved, the more fully must this ideal be approximated.

Frequently, those individuals who would be among the prime targets of experimentation, in terms of the policies being tested, will be indi-

30. Ibid.

31. See Katz, *Experimentation with Human Beings,* pp. 609–73, for a full discussion of these problems.

32. In HEW's income maintenance experiment a random sample of 141 families were given the right to obtain their monthly grant approximately three weeks in advance of the payment date. The objective of this trial was to see how participants behaved when given access to ready cash for emergency situations. In a cautiously worded letter they were told that they would be charged a monthly interest rate of 4 percent on the advance (with a minimum charge of $4 per advance) if they chose to use it. The program was discontinued after five months because of abnormally high use—25 percent of the participants requested advances at least once during a four-month period. Furthermore, it was apparent that participants tended to use the advance for budgeting purposes rather than as a source of funds for emergencies. Stanford Research Institute, memorandums (1973); and Mathematica, Inc., memorandums (1973).

viduals who are particularly prone to undue inducements. Moreover, in some experimental situations monetary inducements may not pose as significant a problem as the threats that the potential subject believes the institution operating the experiment holds over him. Under these circumstances extra care in securing consent is required.[33]

Before leaving the issues surrounding adults who participate in experiments, it is necessary to make it clear why these arguments do not call into question many legal institutions based on consenting. From a legal point of view it is usually taken as an operational rule that persons can consent on their own behalf. Many of society's functions such as marriage and the ability to contract are based on this assumption. The law necessarily deals with general situations and hence must employ rules that can be accepted for the most part. However, applying these rules, *in particular cases,* may be immoral[34]—that is, while it may be legal to secure and act on someone's consent, it may also be immoral. *In enrolling subjects in experiments, simple reliance on legally binding forms of consent may lead to involving persons who are not truly able to consent. This standard does not necessarily apply to other legal institutions based on consent.*

In many of the current social experiments the government because of its sovereign immunity may be in an unusual position. Hence, some of the usual legal protections accorded to the parties in a consent relationship may be absent, or at least diminished, unless safeguards are built into experimental procedures themselves.[35]

Limitations on Consenting for Children

The OEO experiment in performance contracting for education required the consent of parents before a student was included in one of the experimental classes (this requirement was apparently not always met).[36] The experiment raises the question of whether obtaining parental consent eliminates the need for further concern about possible harm to the child.

33. For a detailed analysis of the ethical problems associated with differential power between experimenter and subject, see Herbert C. Kelman, "The Rights of the Subject in Social Research: An Analysis in Terms of Relative Power and Legitimacy," *American Psychologist,* vol. 27 (November 1972), pp. 989–1016.

34. Aristotle discusses the importance of the distinction between the lawful and the just in *Ethics,* bk. 5, chap. 10.

35. For a brief discussion of federal government immunity, see William L. Prosser, *Handbook of the Law of Torts* (West, 1971), pp. 970–75.

36. For a review of the legal aspects of the experiment, see Reed Martin, "Performance Contracting: Making It Legal," *Nation's Schools,* January 1971, pp. 62–64.

The hazards of an educational philosophy that differs significantly from the parent's are not at issue since presumably the parent would not consent if the experiments rested on philosophies that were antagonistic to his own. Performance contracting, however, introduces another possible harm. Since the contractor is paid on the basis of the number of children who reach a minimum standard on reading and mathematical tests, and on how well they do, he is likely to concentrate on those children he thinks he can improve the most. Those the contractor believes to be least educable run the risk of receiving less instruction and actually falling behind, and those who appear to need education the least risk being neglected because they will probably achieve high test scores without special instruction. Does the parent have the right to consent to the participation of his child in such an experiment if he has reason to believe that his child will be one of those the contractor could neglect?

Ordinary moral intuition indicates that there should be a two-tiered test at this point, one having to do with the parent's customary responsibilities and the other with peculiar prerogatives of the parent. Generally, a parent's authority over his child does not extend to cases where the child is made significantly worse off.[37] This is the basis for laws against child neglect and abuse, as well as compulsory school attendance laws.[38] It is not considered socially desirable that parents' rights over children extend to circumstances where the children will suffer a serious failure to cultivate basic skills for getting along in society.[39] This is at least one of the reasons why the state takes on the responsibility of providing free and universal public education and why parents of children who are not ade-

---

37. See, for instance, *Prince* v. *Massachusetts,* 321 U.S. 158 (1944). Of course, a parent is permitted under many circumstances to make a child worse off (more unhappy) in the short run in order to promote his long-term interests. Whether this argument could be used here will depend on how these neglected children fare, though it is difficult to see how they could be better off in the long or short run.

38. However, there are several cases where the parent's authority is permitted to extend to circumstances where the child is made worse off, though even here there are limits. Where there are constitutionally guaranteed liberties to the adult, parents are granted wider latitude. For example, in *Wisconsin* v. *Yoder,* 40 U.S.L.W. 4476 (1972), Amish parents claimed that state laws that required school attendance until age 16 were a violation of their freedom of religion. Because of the constitutional guarantees concerning freedom of religion, and the character of the Amish life for which the children were being prepared, the court held that compulsory attendance beyond the eighth grade for these children was unconstitutional.

39. To argue that the parent has the right to consent to procedures where the child is harmed, on the basis of the assumption that the parent is best suited to protect the interests of his child, is absurd.

quately housed and clothed are regarded as legally and morally in default and guilty of child neglect.[40]

In the overwhelming number of cases, parents act to maximize their children's welfare, not diminish it. For parents who consent where there is a substantial chance that their children will be neglected and their education materially retarded or neglected, the consent doctrine is over-extended.

In the case of compulsory attendance laws, parents' discretion on how their children are to be treated is severely limited. This requirement would be morally vacuous if it permitted parents to place their children in learning environments where their education would be neglected.[41]

In performance contracting and similar experiments in education, children who would suffer from induced harms or risks should be excluded from the sample, or an incentive system should be created for the contractor so that it would not be to his benefit to neglect these children. Of course, such an incentive system would have to be examined to discover whether it had scientific merit or any additional perverse consequences.

The Consent Doctrine and Nonparticipants

Some of the moral issues that arise in respect to nonparticipants are evident in the housing allowance supply experiment. That experiment was designed to

"generate information about housing market effects" by "replicating a full scale national housing allowance program in each of two contrasting, medium-sized SMSA's with populations between 200,000 and 250,000.". . . The data gathered in the surveys (to be conducted during the experiment) will relate primarily to questions on supply responsiveness and impact on families not receiving allowances.[42]

In this, a saturation experiment, everyone in the cities chosen with

40. Paul Ramsey states the rule in regard to medical experiments with children as follows: "where there is no possible relation to the child's recovery, a child is not to be made a mere object in medical experimentation for the sake of good to come." *The Patient as Person* (Yale University Press, 1970), p. 12.

41. I do not address the question of whether there might be additional reasons for unusual protections for children. Putting aside the issue of the limits of parental authority, it might be immoral to harm or fail to benefit children because they are children—that is, because they are innocent, partially nondeliberative, and so forth.

42. Robert Beckman, "The Experimental Housing Allowance Program," *Journal of Housing*, vol. 30 (January 1973), p. 15.

suitable family and income characteristics will receive a housing allowance. One of the main questions is how these allowances change suppliers' responses to changed demand conditions. Is supply increased or improved, or is the response primarily one of raising prices?

Regardless of what the response is, some individuals not participating in the experiment will be made worse off. These individuals fall into two groups: those above the income cut-off line, and those below it who are excluded from participation by other rules—rules that operate, for example, against single persons. The latter are perhaps injured the most because their ability to compete in the market could be substantially less than those above the income notch. Those persons just above the point of income ineligibility are placed at a disadvantage in the market because they are faced with a new group of competitors for the same housing. If prices go up, they must either reduce their standards or increase their expenditures. If prices stand still, they will have to wait longer to satisfy their needs. (The experimental design calls for observation of the harm suffered by these individuals. Hence, it is expected that they could be made worse off.)[43]

No attempt has been made to obtain the express (and informed) consent of persons so affected.[44] Since individual consent is impractical, the most plausible method of gaining consent would be a referendum among the individuals in the jurisdictions affected by the market changes. However, express consent need not be sought through referendum or other devices when the ability to grant consent is contained in the express powers of a governing body that can be asked to approve an experiment, or when the customary powers or practices of the governing body approximate express power.

Where the governing body's power is inexact, the obligation to obtain the consent of the nonparticipants cannot be avoided on the grounds that they have already tacitly consented, as citizens and voters in the community in question or in the United States as a whole. Tacit consent is not a legitimate basis for conducting saturation experiments.

John Locke, in the classic statement of the tacit consent position, defines

what ought to be looked upon as a tacit consent, and how far it binds, i.e.,

---

43. If the experiment is phased in slowly so as to permit supply to increase, these problems may be diminished.

44. The designers of the experiment have asked the city councils of the communities in question to agree to the experiment.

how far anyone shall be looked on to have consented, and thereby submitted to any government, where he has made no expressions of it at all. And to this I say that every man that hath any possession or enjoyment of any part of the dominions of any government doth thereby give his tacit consent, and is as far forth obliged to obedience to the laws of that government during such enjoyment as anyone under it; whether this his possession be of land to him and his heirs for ever, or a lodging only for a week; or whether it be barely traveling freely on the highway; and in effect it reaches as far as the very being of anyone within the territories of that government.[45]

Locke's argument is that presence by choice in a political society amounts to an agreement to abide by its laws.

Such tacit consent is not sufficient justification for saturation experiments that may cause harm to nonparticipants. For, if tacit consent can be read so broadly as to include the individual's agreement to novel procedures in an experiment that are adverse to such substantive areas of personal interest as the cost of housing, then consent would establish the legitimacy of nothing since it would establish the legitimacy of everything. If it can be presumed that a person agrees to circumstances that make him worse off, then tacit consent becomes a potential justification for the most unreasonable kinds of treatment.

The tacit consent implied in the approval of a city council or other public body, as a grantor of consent on the part of the citizens,[46] does not extend to novel experiments. Consent involves the creating of rights in an agent; it is not a blanket authorization, however, to act on behalf of another. In some cases the limits of these rights are clearly enumerated, and in others they follow usual and customary practice. The newness of the federal experiments, and the fact that the consequences of the housing allowance experiment are difficult to predict, or even unknown, would seem to rule out appeals to usual and customary practice. It is not in the express powers of the charters of the cities in question to permit authorization of such an experiment.[47] Tacit consent does not involve consent to

45. "Essay Concerning Civil Government," pp. 451–52.
46. This approach was used in the housing supply experiment, and some of the appropriate governing bodies in the sample area refused consent. Insofar as the procedure was justified to begin with, this would rule out the experiment in those areas since those communities will still be feeling the adverse price effects of the allowances.
47. For example, according to the State of Michigan's Municipal Corporations Act (M.S.A. sec. 5.2073[j], 1973), "Each city charter shall provide: (j) for the public peace and health and for the safety of persons and property." Whether this general statement regarding the powers of cities provides them with the authority to undertake saturation-type experiments, such as the housing allowance experi-

novel kinds of decisions. For these same reasons, getting the approval of school or other public officials for the performance contracting experiments may not be sufficient to establish their legitimacy.

Perhaps this point may be seen more clearly by imagining the following absurd use of tacit consent arguments. The city council of X municipality permits the Air Force to test a new atomic device by dropping it on the city. One of the few survivors staggers up to a city council member and blurts: "What happened?" The city council member replies that the council authorized the test on the basis of the "tacit consent" of the citizens of the city. Since nothing in the charter prohibited such authorization, it was presumed that the citizens consented to it. Clearly, such a reply would be absurd. The point is that tacit consent cannot be *presumed* to establish the legitimacy of noncustomary actions or actions (which involve risk or harm) that are not expressly authorized.

Nor can tacit consent to actions of the federal government that have been approved by Congress and the executive branch be used to justify saturation experiments. The tacit consent theory of political obligation is unacceptable in modern political systems, according to Wertheimer, because "the populations of such systems are quite large."[48]

Groups of different size are distinguished (of course, not exclusively) by their "interaction possibilities," for interactions which occur in small groups "inevitably disappear when the groups grow larger." Consent is one such "interaction possibility" which disappears when groups grow larger. . . . In the face-to-face context it was possible to show how persons can be asked for their consent, how consent is (or is not) given voluntarily, and how it can be communicated verbally or nonverbally. When the conditions are met, the act of consent changes people's mutual expectations and creates a moral relationship. The size of the modern nation, however, precludes the interactions that consent requires. No one can give consent because no one is in a position to note whether or not it has been given. . . . To say "I consent to my political system" in the modern polity is like saying "I do thee wed" when one is alone. It is an absurd act, and has about the same consequences: None.

As the size of collectivities to which we belong increases, and as the members of those collectivities become more remote, we nevertheless continue to employ the concepts that we use in understanding and relating to those in the more immediate environment. In attempting to describe political relationships

---

ment, which affect a class of citizens in the city, is not clear and may eventually be subject to litigation.

48. Alan P. Wertheimer, "Political Coercion and Political Obligation," in J. Roland Pennock and John W. Chapman, eds., *Coercion*, NOMOS series, vol. 14 (Lieber-Atherton, Inc., © 1972), p. 220. Wertheimer believes the arguments apply to express consent as well.

in terms of consent, we have transferred a concept from the "face-to-face" context to the political context and have assumed that this could be done without any significant loss in meaning. It does not work.[49]

This argument is directly applicable to the housing allowance experiment because the normal conventions—formal contracts, words, facial expressions, and gestures—that signal consent in small groups do not exist between individuals in a remote city and a large federal bureaucracy. This is what makes Locke's argument (at least in respect to tacit consent) unapplicable to the modern state. To make this argument applicable to the housing experiment would require some appropriate communication signaling consent between the residents of the two cities and the federal establishment, especially the Department of Housing and Urban Development.

Neither is it possible to rely on an argument like Locke's that presence in a political jurisdiction is sufficient signal of consent. For, as Wertheimer argues, "membership in political systems is involuntary, unselective, and coercive."[50]

I do not think it difficult to show that political systems are both involuntary and coercive. . . . I suppose that residence in a political system is more voluntary than residence in a prison—escape is easier, although only for some. Even if one is legally able to leave a political system, many persons lack the economic mobility to make emigration a remote possibility. And unlike a prison, the alternative to residence in one political system is residence in another. . . . If it were the case that residence in a political system were voluntary, the problem of its moral justification would not even arise. The problem of political obligation would not be a problem.

The claim that political systems employ coercion requires even less discussion. While it is certainly true that political systems do seek and obtain compliance through utilitarian and normative techniques, as Max Weber has stated, it is the distinctive characteristic of political systems that "the enforcement of its order is carried out continually within a given territorial area by the application and threat of physical force." . . . it seems fair to assume that when we speak of political systems, we speak of systems that do employ coercive power in creating conformity with its norms.[51]

This description of the involuntariness of political behavior may not, of course, apply to all citizens. It is certainly possible for some individuals to move from the United States or from the communities involved in the housing experiment. What may be reasonably feasible for a small number

49. Ibid., pp. 220–21.
50. Ibid., p. 220.
51. Ibid., pp. 227–28.

of relatively mobile individuals, however, may not be feasible for many of the persons affected by the housing experiment. Many of them do not have the financial means necessary for travel, resettlement, and job search; indeed, many of them may be at or near the poverty level. To describe the presence of these people in a jurisdiction as voluntary is inaccurate.

It follows that attempts to provide moral legitimacy for saturation experiments by reference to tacit informed consent cannot be presumed to be valid. If community governments give their approval to such experiments, such approval must rest on their express powers or be within the scope of customary practice.

The use of informed consent requires caution in social experiments. This is true both for individuals within the sample in nonsaturation experiments and for individuals within and outside the sample in saturation experiments. Moreover, the more individuals are placed at risk in an experiment, the more attention must be paid to the characteristics of the individual being asked to consent.

Experiments in the Public Interest

Under certain circumstances, the rights of individuals affected by an experiment may be abridged. The knowledge gained in such experiments may be valued both for its own sake and because it is believed to be instrumental in the formulation of public policy. When can the importance of this knowledge serve as a basis for setting aside individual rights? To put the question most sharply, when could an experiment like the housing supply experiment be justified, even though persons within the sample refused to give their consent and persons outside the sample had not consented?

The answer to these questions must accord with normal reflective moral intuitions. In analogous circumstances, such moral decisions coalesce around the notion of systemic collapse of essential services or industries, or substantial damage to the public safety.[52] In such disparate areas as mandatory vaccination,[53] internment of citizens,[54] seizure of

52. As Paul Ramsey suggests in "Screening: An Ethicist's View" in Bruce Hilton and others, *Ethical Issues in Human Genetics* (Plenum, 1973), p. 149, perhaps these arguments can be derived from consent, by supposing that in respect to issues of survival everyone would consent to suspension of customary moral rules.

53. *Jacobson* v. *Commonwealth of Massachusetts,* 197 U.S. 11 (1904).

54. *Korematsu* v. *United States,* 323 U.S. 214 (1945).

diseased livestock,[55] and compulsory service in the armed forces (the draft is justified on the grounds of compelling national interest), the judicial legislative rulemaking suggests that the abridgment of the rights of individuals is justified not by reference to the aggregate increase of happiness, but by a substantive threat to an environmental or social system.[56]

Thus social experiments that involve risks, harm, or the substantive invasion of privacy for persons within the sample whose ability to consent is impaired (including children) must pass this same sort of test, unless those individuals can somehow be protected. Where the experiments involve risks, harm, or the substantive invasion of privacy for persons outside the sample, the consent of these individuals cannot be presumed. If these experiments cannot gain the legitimate consent of all affected parties, they should be ruled out, unless failure to perform them would impair crucial environmental or social systems.

COMMENTS BY JOSEPH P. NEWHOUSE

Brown argues that a certain type of person exists for whom the consent doctrine is inappropriate. The characteristics that distinguish such an individual are his short time frame and his poverty. The individual's time frame is relevant because an experimenter may ask him to consent to undertake actions whose adverse effects would occur beyond his time horizon, so that he is not capable of considering them in the decision to participate. In this case, informed consent cannot exist. Poverty is relevant, according to Brown, because there may be undue inducement for the poor to participate; consent cannot then be freely given.

Brown presents no evidence that a group in the society exists that is incapable of considering consequences over the relevant time frame. If such a group does not exist, much of his argument is irrelevant. If his assertion is correct, then too much is proved, for his argument implies that some of society's basic institutions have fundamental flaws.

Many of society's institutions are built around the notion that individuals are, if not competent to judge their own futures, at least less error-prone in this respect than any other person.[57] If this were not so, pre-

---

55. Food and Drug Act, *United States Code,* title 21, sec. 134(a).

56. For a more extended review of such considerations, see pp. 127–63, below.

57. Less error-prone in the same sense that a certain estimator has minimum mean-square error. Brown's quote from Mill (p. 84, above) makes the same point.

sumably there would be considerably more restrictions placed on actions of the individual, especially his freedom to contract. Individuals are free, for example, to enlist in the armed services for periods up to four years, to borrow money from a loan company or bank (albeit they cannot borrow at usurious interest rates), and to procreate and rear children. While freedom to contract is not unlimited (as Brown points out, they cannot sell themselves into slavery), it would be inconsistent with the rights accorded the individual in other contexts to take from him the right to participate in a social experiment. In the case of the social experiment the individual is not even making a contract in the sense of enlisting in the military or borrowing money, since he is free to withdraw from the experiment.

There is, of course, one group on whom significant restrictions are placed. That is the institutionalized population. (None of the current social experiments attempts to enroll the institutionalized population.) Brown's argument that there is a group of individuals who are incapable of consenting implies that they should be treated like the institutionalized population. To me this proves too much.

My argument can be made concrete by reference to the health insurance experiment. Brown argues that it is inappropriate to enroll individuals in this experiment who do not have a sufficiently long time horizon to judge the risks to their health. However, all individuals who are considered eligible for the experiment could engage in hazardous occupations for relatively high rates of pay; moreover, all of them are permitted to smoke and consume alcoholic beverages. These activities are likely to impair their health more significantly than any change in the consumption of medical services while they are enrolled in the experiment, the more so since the reimbursement scheme enables them to buy more of any kind of medical services than they could otherwise buy.[58] The logic of Brown's argument is that these individuals are not able to and should not be allowed to make trade-offs between various desirable goals, including health status. It is precisely such trade-offs that are being made when individuals choose not to buckle their seat belts or choose a diet made up of foods low in nutritional value. Again, it is only the institutionalized population that is not permitted to make this kind of trade-off.

In sum, Brown has presented no evidence to support his assertion that

58. On the connection between these activities and health, see particularly Victor R. Fuchs, *Who Shall Live? Health, Economics, and Social Choice* (Basic Books, 1974).

a group with a short time horizon exists. Moreover, his conclusion from this assertion—that restrictions should be placed on the freedom of individuals to enroll in an experiment—appears inconsistent with the rights and privileges that the noninstitutionalized population enjoys.

Brown's second argument is that for the poor the inducement to participate constitutes an exertion of "undue power and influence," that the individual who confronts an "extremely attractive" offer cannot be said to have "freely" consented. One logical implication would be that if the poor are to participate in an experiment, they should be paid less than the well-to-do. This seems an extraordinary conclusion, but so is the proposition it is based on. Why should not an individual be free to make a transaction that will greatly benefit him? What justification is there for a standard that holds that the greater the benefit, the less moral the transaction? Perhaps it is that if a rational individual is making so large an offer, he is presumably asking the person to undertake considerable effort or risk. If so, one must assume the poor person's ability to assess this effort or risk, and it is this ability that Brown apparently doubts. But again the answer is that society's institutions presume that the individual can make such judgments in many other endeavors; to maintain that he cannot in this case is to argue that society's mechanisms for institutionalization have failed.

Brown's arguments about enrollment of children in experiments also imply that society's institutions are malfunctioning. These institutions presume that parents are competent to judge their children's welfare—to the degree required by any of the experiments Brown discusses. For example, the parents decide when medical treatment should be sought for the child, and what type of medical insurance they ought to obtain for their children. Brown's example is the performance contracting experiment. He questions whether the parent has the right to consent to his child's participation "if he has reason to believe that his child will be one of those the contractor will neglect." There are so many choices made by the parent that affect the child's welfare to the degree this one does that it appears unreasonable to concentrate on it. Furthermore, Brown makes no mention of the child's alternatives. If these are sufficiently bad, the parent may sensibly opt for a contractor who would neglect the child.[59]

59. In fact, Brown seems to compare performance contracting with an ideal system rather than the actual educational system. He finds it outrageous that some parents were not given the opportunity to consent on behalf of their children. While granting that this would have been a preferable and feasible course, my sense of outrage is tempered by the lack of control parents have over public school curriculum generally, not to mention the amount of attention any particular child gets from his teachers.

In sum, society presumes a parent is competent to judge for his children at the level of choice that the experiments under review call on the parents to make. If the parent cannot be presumed to be competent to make this choice, then society's institutions for child rearing are called into question.

Brown identifies another group of individuals for whom the consent doctrine is inappropriate. They are those who do not participate in the experiment but are affected by its outcome. He points out that the housing allowance supply experiment may so inflate costs in the local housing market that nonparticipants will be forced to pay more for housing. He argues that the express and informed consent of these individuals ought to be obtained, and suggests that a referendum be held among them, which would be decided by majority vote. Moreover, such individuals should be compensated for any losses they may suffer. Brown goes on to assert that tacit consent to saturation experiments cannot be presumed to make them valid.

The problem with Brown's argument is that any new public program can be viewed as a saturation experiment for the entire country. Thus, it would appear that much of public policy is not legitimate. Again Brown is in the position of having proved too much.

Brown tries to distinguish experimentation from policy on several grounds, arguing that an experiment selects a limited sample—that is, that it is not universal. This is, of course, true, but none of Brown's arguments seem affected by it. His argument that tacit consent is not legitimate should apply equally to those adversely affected by public policy (for example, workers who are unemployed because of a tariff reduction).

Brown also tries to distinguish an experiment from policy on the grounds that an experiment is a new program whose consequences are unknown. But obviously there are many new public programs whose consequences are unknown. The urban renewal program and the interstate highway program are two whose consequences are widely thought to have been unanticipated. Indeed, one might question whether the consequences of any major new public program have been entirely foreseen. Thus, there is no essential difference between experiments and policy for the purpose of Brown's argument.[60]

60. One might attempt to distinguish certain experiments that deliberately exaggerate a treatment beyond the range that might be considered feasible for policy in order to measure what, if any, effects might be caused by the treatment (none of the experiments Brown discusses, in my opinion, does this). It is not clear, even in such experiments, that a different decision process from that applied to any public program is called for.

Brown suggests that normal majoritarian collective procedures are not adequate to judge experiments—that in the housing experiment it is not sufficient to obtain the consent of the city council in the affected area, and that a referendum should be held. But under current political institutions, decisions are generally delegated to elected representatives. Brown argues that newness precludes this, but this would appear to imply that any new program should be submitted to a referendum. A more defensible argument would be that a program that affects substantial numbers of nonparticipants (a saturation experiment) ought to be approved by a representative body at the local level (in the housing experiment, the city councils or metropolitan governments would appear appropriate). Whether compensation should be paid—and, if so, how—is a more difficult question, and one probably not susceptible to a priori solution.

In sum, Brown has two principal points, neither of which appears consistent with present social institutions. The first is that a group of individuals incapable of consenting exists; this group is either not sufficiently perceptive or too poor to make wise decisions. In some respects, this is a simple argument about paternalism. I believe that this group's exclusion from offers to participate in experiments would imply that society's mechanisms for institutionalization have failed. Brown's second point is that nonparticipants who are affected by an experiment ought to have the right to disapprove of it and ought to be compensated for harm done them. I have argued that there is nothing to distinguish an experiment from other kinds of decisions that duly constituted representatives are called on to make, and that a special referendum is therefore not called for. It would also appear consistent with other public policy decision making to let the amount and kind of compensation, if any, be decided by the elected body.

EDWARD M. GRAMLICH

LARRY L. ORR

The Ethics
of Social Experimentation

The recent large-scale social experiments sponsored by various government agencies have raised for social scientists certain ethical issues that have long confronted researchers in other fields. Under what circumstances is it ethical to experiment with people's lives and welfare? How should people be enticed to participate in an experiment and compensated for any harm done them by the experiment? When are the benefits of the experiment sizable enough that the government might risk injury to a few participants in the enterprise? How and at what cost should the government try to minimize these risks? Is ethical behavior at all inconsistent with the research quality of the experiment? Social scientists are generally a pragmatic bunch and in the early large-scale experiments they have answered these questions as best they could, without discussing them in any systematic way. But as the number of experiments grows and the ethical issues become more complicated, it becomes increasingly important that social scientists conduct such a systematic discussion.

Ethical Standards of Experimentation

In experimentation, as in all of its activities, the government has a fundamental ethical obligation to protect the rights and welfare of individuals affected by its actions. In its normal policymaking operations the government is deemed free to carry out activities that harm individuals or groups of individuals as long as, in the process of doing this, it is trying to maximize some concept of collective social welfare and it does not violate certain fundamental rights of individual citizens. Thus the government would be free to impose a tariff that would harm certain groups (consumers) as long as it felt that aggregate national welfare would be improved in the process. But it would not be ethical for the government to try to achieve the same end by curtailing certain basic rights of individuals such as freedom or the right of voluntary association and contract.

Experiments raise somewhat different ethical issues because they are designed not as statutory policies but as devices to gain information. Since the population affected by the experiment is then in a sense incidental to the main point of the enterprise, and also because of the flexibility in design and sample selection available to experimenters, it has become customary to insist that government social policy experiments satisfy a more stringent ethical standard. This standard, similar to that used in medical experiments, maintains that experiments are ethical if subjects voluntarily give their consent to participate, as long as the experimenter gives the subjects all the information they need to act in their own long-run best interests and informs them of their right to drop out of the experiment at any time. Under these conditions of voluntary, informed consent, the individual participant perceives at all times a positive change in his welfare due to the experiment—otherwise he would not agree to participate or to remain enrolled. The experiment can be thought of as satisfying a perpetual market test because the participants are always valuing the expected benefits of continued participation more than the costs.

The standard of voluntary, informed consent is more protective of the welfare of individual citizens than the standards of private legal contracts in two different ways. On the one hand, the government sanctions legal transactions entailing far greater risks than those involved in most social experiments on the grounds that an individual should be free to make those agreements he views as advantageous even if in the end they prove otherwise. On the other hand, unlike private contracts, social experiments allow participants to withdraw, and thus revoke their consent, at any time.

The protection against harm provided by voluntary consent does not, of course, eliminate all personal risk in an experiment. Social experiments deal with treatments that have uncertain effects on subjects, hence raising the very important distinction between expected risks and actual losses. The fact that subjects willingly agree to participate and to remain enrolled means that at any time they view the expected benefits of continued participation as outweighing the costs of any harm done them. It does not mean that no harm will be done them, for this is the nature of uncertainty. Such uncertainty should not rule out experimentation, but it should lead the prudent experimenter to try to minimize the likelihood of personal losses in the design of the experiment.

The requirement that the experimenter give all the information subjects need to act in their own long-run best interests poses difficulties because the treatments in most social experiments may not be well understood by the subjects. Should the experimenter read through a long legal description of the subjects' precise rights and prerogatives in a given experiment, or should he try to simplify this description to deal with only those points that might be of practical relevance? On the one hand, he does not want to usurp the subjects' decision-making power, as so often happens when well-meaning people deal with the poor, but on the other hand he does not want to give subjects so much information that they fail to perceive the central questions. Whatever the case, it follows that experimenters have no moral obligation to give subjects more information than they need to act in their long-run best interests, particularly if there is a risk that subjects might respond differently if they only knew they were being studied (as the well-known Hawthorne effect might suggest).

A final difficulty in interpreting the accepted condition of experimental ethics concerns whether subjects understand their own consent to the experiment. Peter Brown argues that it is unethical to allow subjects to participate in experiments even if they consent to it if they are incapable of seeing far enough into the future to understand how the experiment will affect them. Brown's extension of the accepted definition raises the question of whether, in protecting short-sighted people from social experimenters, it is in turn a violation of their freedom to prevent them from participating in an experiment even if they want to for irrational reasons. This protection may be just as undemocratic as having the experimenter "simplify" a description of the rights and prerogatives of poor individuals. Beyond this, short of some new and unexpected psychological break-throughs, it will never be possible to determine whether a particular subject does in fact understand what he is consenting to, and therefore whether the experiment is in fact ethical. The issue of whether consent is informed or not, and therefore whether the experiment is ethical or not, thus becomes essentially impossible to resolve.

For this reason, Brown's extended definition of consent simply cannot be used as an operational guide. Under it, a policymaker who tried to behave in an assuredly ethical manner would not be able to do any experiments at all. While this may be the most assuredly ethical way to proceed, it is generally not the best way to proceed. If there really is substantial uncertainty about the effect of policy, it is far more responsible to design and conduct an experiment with alternative programs to find out the benefits and costs of a policy than simply to proceed with a national program without this knowledge.

The narrow definition of consent is just that, however, and may create certain problems. Even people who are capable of consenting may have blind spots or irrationalities, especially if they are the uneducated, low-income people who are likely to be the subjects for most social experiments. Thus, while the narrow definition of consent ought to be used in social experiments, government experimenters should lean over backward to minimize any ex post injuries or difficulties that may result from the uninformed consent of certain subjects.[1] With appropriate safeguards, experimenters operating under the narrow definition, and thus allowed to do experiments that would not be prima facie unethical, would not be causing much harm even when their work is measured by a more stringent ethical standard.

To Do or Not to Do the Experiment

Under what circumstances should the government risk the ethical difficulties entailed in social experiments in order to gain the presumably larger benefits of the information generated by an experiment? The decision should be based on a comparison of the experiment's benefits and costs, where both are defined to include any welfare gains or losses of participants (or others affected by the experiment). On the one hand, this rule permits experiments to be done even if they could cause harm to some participants if the benefits are great enough; on the other hand, it will turn out that both ethical considerations and research considerations argue for designing experiments in such a way that the risk of harm to participants is as slight as possible.

The main benefit of an experiment consists of the information gained about some behavioral response to policy (labor supply, utilization of medical care, demand for housing, improvement in educational test scores). With this information, the government will be better able to devise policies that bring about desired levels of income support, consumption of certain goods or services, educational improvement, or whatever.

1. This additional ethical constraint on social experiments would have the same practical effect as Charles Schultze's principle of increasing marginal harm. See pp. 120–21, below.

The research value of the experiment then depends on the degree to which the experiment reduces uncertainty about relevant behavioral responses along with some measure of the welfare cost of suboptimal policies.

Apart from its effects on the participants directly involved, the normal benefit-cost calculation would suggest that an experiment should be done if its research value is greater than its budgetary cost, but not otherwise.[2] Such a standard is difficult to apply, because the benefits involve both uncertainty and a judgment of the importance of people's consumption deficiencies in certain areas. But this difficulty is not obviously any more serious with experiments than with social policies. If the government is willing to plow ahead with intuitive, political benefit-cost judgments for legislative policies, it should do the same for experiments.

From the point of view of the individual, the application of voluntary consent procedures insures that each and every participant must view the ex ante benefits of participation as positive. It follows that the net participation benefits for all subjects taken together will also be positive. Thus in deciding whether or not to do an experiment, the government can safely ignore a calculation of the net participation benefits of subjects, because the subjects themselves in agreeing to participate will have accepted the experiment on these grounds. Though it would be stretching the point, one could even argue that a pure research benefit-cost calculation is biased against the experiment because it ignores the positive ex ante net benefits of participants.

While calculation of the net benefits of participants may seem of only academic interest, in practice this is probably the most extensively debated ethical question in social experiments. Since these experiments have usually dealt with the provision of services to the needy, the main question asked by representatives of the local population is more likely to be why more people cannot be included in the experiment than it is to be whether people should or should not participate. In other words, they assume that ex ante benefits are positive and want them to be extended to more people, or at least to more needy people. If the expectations underlying this view are realistic, then concern about the ethical problems of experimentation may be misplaced.[3]

2. For an analysis of the benefit-cost calculation, see Larry L. Orr, "Optimal Scale in Social Experimentation" (March 1972; processed).

3. The problem of denying needy people experimental treatments would only be an ethical problem in the strictest sense if the experimenter knew the treatment to be beneficial. If he were certain, there would be no point in an experimental test of the treatment.

Even though all participants in an experiment expect positive net benefits, nonparticipants who may be affected by the experiment but whose consent is not secured do not. Most large-scale experiments to date have probably imposed only trivial costs on nonparticipants, but such costs may become important in some future experiments. In the housing allowance supply experiment, for example, it is likely that housing prices and rents will be driven up throughout the cities of the experiment, which will make worse off all median- and high-income nonparticipants who are bidding for the same stock of housing. In such cases some form of the principle of consent should be extended to those nonparticipants who are likely to be affected. It is difficult to determine just how this should be done, because it may be impossible to exclude people living in a certain area from the impact of the experiment even if they want to be excluded; at a minimum, experimenters should obtain the consent of the elected representatives of these affected nonparticipants. In this way the experiment can at least satisfy the consensus ethical standard for affected nonparticipants as a group, if not individually.[4]

Research considerations also argue for minimizing risk to participants. If the experiment contains extreme risks or does not look appealing for any other reason, the rate of refusal to participate or the rate of attrition is likely to be high. As a consequence, the experimental sample would be less representative of the subject population as a whole and the results of the experiment correspondingly less useful. Experimenters might try to minimize refusals and attrition by higher cash incentives for participation, but this will lead to greater budgetary costs, which again makes the experiment less desirable from a research standpoint.

Ethical Issues in the Health Insurance Experiment

The social experimenter's ethical obligation to attempt to minimize ex post welfare losses, as well as to design treatments that will be viewed by participants as a net welfare gain ex ante, often raises significant design and operational issues. The health insurance experiment illustrates the

4. This extension of the consent principle may not always have the intended effect. When representatives of the Department of Housing and Urban Development took their proposal for a housing allowance supply experiment before the city council of Green Bay, Wisconsin, and carefully explained that local house prices might increase as a result, the council's immediate response was eagerly to calculate the implicit rise in property tax revenues. Such is democracy.

types of ethical problems and possible solutions involved in experimentation.[5]

Participants in the health insurance study are to be given an insurance policy that provides for reimbursement of medical expenses for a comprehensive range of covered services, with varying levels of deductibles and coinsurance. The experimental plans range from full-coverage policies (with no deductibles or coinsurance), through plans with 25 percent and 50 percent coinsurance rates, to plans with substantial deductibles. In all plans, however, medical expenses are to be fully reimbursed once the family's medical expenditures reach a specified fraction of family income.

A major objective of the study is to ascertain the effects of various degrees of cost-sharing on the demand for medical care. Therefore, it is necessary to require that participants forgo benefits from any existing health insurance plans they may hold, so that they will be reacting only to the terms of the experimental policy. This raises the possibility that families might be made financially worse off by accepting an experimental plan with cost-sharing requirements that provides substantially less benefits than their existing insurance.

To guard against this possibility, the experimental design includes periodic cash payments to the participants, calculated to insure that even in the worst possible case, each family will suffer no financial loss from participation. The "worst possible case" under the experimental plans is that in which the family's cost-sharing liability reaches its limit. To calculate the family's annual cash payment, this figure is reduced by the cost-sharing liability the family would have incurred at that level of total expenditures under the most generous provisions of its existing insurance (typically the hospitalization provisions) and the premium paid by the family for that insurance. The remainder is to be paid to the family in periodic cash installments.[6] Since these cash payments will be made to participants without regard to their actual consumption of medical care, most families will end up financially better off than under their existing coverage. No family will be worse off.

---

5. A more complete catalogue of questions regarding the health insurance experiment, sponsored by the Department of Health, Education, and Welfare, can be found in Joseph P. Newhouse, "A Design for a Health Insurance Experiment," *Inquiry,* March 1974, pp. 5–27.

6. These are lump-sum payments which should not affect the family's demand for medical care except through their effect on total family income. The analysis is designed to measure, and adjust for, any such effects.

Special procedures have also been developed to avoid harm connected with the termination of the experiment. Since it was quite likely that at least a few participants would become medically uninsurable during the course of the experiment, and thus would face a substantial ex post welfare loss, they were not asked to drop their existing coverage upon enrollment. Instead, existing coverage is to be kept in force throughout the experiment. The experiment will pay any premiums for these policies, and encourage participants to take advantage of new coverage opportunities they may become eligible for (say, because of a job change), but the participants will agree not to file claims against this insurance. Benefits from these policies will be assigned by the families to the experiment, and the experiment will reclaim against the policies as claims are filed with the experiment. Reclaimed benefits should cover the cost of premium payments to keep the nonexperimental policies in force.

A more subtle ethical problem concerns the possibility that participants who face high coinsurance rates under the experiment may underconsume medical care, to the detriment of their health. The importance of this risk depends, of course, on the magnitude of the actual response to prices, which is the central question under study and is a priori unknown.

The notion of underconsumption of care is itself impossible to define. In the experiment, the choice of how much care to consume remains with the family under the advice of their physician, and unless one is willing to adopt some paternalistic standard of the amount of care families "ought" to consume, it is hard to fault their decisions. Because of the experiment, all families will have higher monetary incomes and thus will be financially able to spend more on health care if they choose. Moreover, they will be protected against medical expenses that are catastrophic in relation to their income. The health insurance risk that participants in the experiment run is not at all unique. They freely choose to accept or reject the experimental coverage just as all families routinely choose various levels of health insurance—or no health insurance at all. Unlike other families, however, participants are free to revoke this choice at any time and return to their prior coverage, regardless of their medical condition. Finally, whatever the risk involved, it is confined to those families whose experimental plan entails higher cost-sharing than the policy they would otherwise hold. Many families in the experiment will receive much better coverage and virtually all will be covered for a more comprehensive scope of services—particularly out-patient and preventive services—than would otherwise be the case. All things considered, underconsumption appears to pose an ethical problem in the health insurance experiment only if one is unwilling to allow participants in an experimental study to make the same kinds of decisions that virtually all families make in the normal course of life.[7]

Providing participants with all the information they need to act in their own long-run best interests is particularly difficult in the health insurance experiment. Compounding the usual experimental intricacies of interviewing, reporting, treatment of family splits, and the like, are the inherent intricacies of health insurance, the arrangements for assignment of benefits from existing coverage, and cash payments. Every attempt is made to present all of these aspects of the experiment fully and honestly, in language the participant can understand. At enrollment, the family is given both oral and written explanations of their rights and obligations under the experiment, including covered medical services, coinsurance provisions and catastrophic coverage, assignment of benefits, their right to revert to existing coverage upon withdrawal or termination, and their obligations to file claims and participate in interviews. A detailed, written comparison of the family's experimental plan and their existing coverage is presented, and the family is invited to defer their decision until they have had time to study these materials, solicit legal or personal advice, or contact any of a list of government officials and community leaders who can vouch for the legitimacy of the experiment. Once a family elects to participate, they are asked to sign an enrollment agreement that details their major rights and responsibilities under the experiment. They are also reminded of their right to take out new nonexperimental insurance at the experiment's expense if they change jobs during the course of the experiment, or to withdraw from the experiment. Nothing in the enrollment agreement binds the family beyond their decision to withdraw from the experiment; the experiment is, however, bound by the terms of the agreement so long as the family continues to participate.

The health insurance experiment also raises questions about experimenters' responsibility to inform participants of facts that have nothing to do with the experimental treatment per se. To obtain necessary baseline data, some of the participants are given physical examinations before be-

7. *The Institutional Guide to DHEW Policy on Protection of Human Subjects* explicitly refuses to go this far: "Certain risks are inherent in life itself, at the time and in the places where life runs its course. This policy is not concerned with the ordinary risks of public or private living." (U.S. Department of Health, Education, and Welfare, Public Health Service and National Institutes of Health, DHEW Publication [NIH] 72-102 [Dec. 1, 1971], p. 2).

ginning the experiment. Should this examination indicate that a participant is in need of immediate medical attention, the experimenter faces a conflict between his scientific objectives on one hand and his ethical obligations on the other. If participants are encouraged to seek care, their health may improve, but the experimental results will be biased. While nobody would take the experiment so seriously as to refuse to inform those who are gravely ill of their need for care, it is most difficult in practice to decide where to draw the line. There could even be a problem in providing subjects too much encouragement to seek health care, if they come to believe that the experiment is taking care of their health and fail to seek diagnostic or preventive care on their own. This issue has been resolved by providing the results of all physical examinations to the participants' physicians; to assess the effect of this examination on the utilization of services, this subgroup will be compared with participants who do not receive physicals.[8]

It is too early to tell how effective these procedures will be. The limited experience with a small pilot sample of families does indicate that they have a reasonably good understanding of their benefits and obligations under the experiment.

While many of the issues encountered in the health insurance experiment are unique to that experiment, they do serve to illustrate several general points. The most important is that the extended definition of consent cannot be used as an operational guide in determining whether or not to do the experiment—if for no other reason than that it is impossible for the experimenter to know whether the participants thoroughly understand how an experiment will affect them in the long run. The only thing he can do is honestly and completely give the subjects all information relevant to their own decision to participate—and even this is a difficult task. Beyond this, the health insurance example illustrates the fact that research objectives and ethical considerations are not necessarily in conflict, for as the necessary cash payments to induce participation are lower, the less is the likelihood of ex post personal losses in the experiment. Finally, the experiment demonstrates how much latitude there is within a social experiment for minimizing these possible ex post losses, and thus satisfying even very stringent ethical standards.

---

8. All subjects will be given physical examinations at the termination of the experiment, and these results, without interpretation, will be given to their physicians. This is an example of how participants could be made better off by virtue of participating.

CHARLES L. SCHULTZE

Social Programs
and Social Experiments

Social experiments are a novel aspect of public policy.
We can seek to derive ethical rules governing their use and abuse directly
from general principles of moral philosophy. But, while necessary, that
approach is very slippery. To bolster our confidence in the rules we derive,
we look for precedents in the ethical rules and procedures already followed in analogous situations. Robert Veatch pursues this approach in his
excellent analysis of the evolution and current status of the rules governing medical experiments using human subjects. But as he recognizes, there
are a number of substantial differences between such medical experiments
and large-scale social experiments.

The inquiry can start also by recognizing that social experiments share
at least some characteristics with operating social programs. There are a
number of rules and procedures, often implicit but nevertheless real, that
society has established to protect human rights in the adoption and execution of social policies and programs. The similarities and the differences
between social programs and social experiments should be instructive.
To what extent do the similarities justify the application to social experiments of the rules and procedures that govern social programs? And to
what extent do the differences require special rules and safeguards for
experiments?

My description of the rules that safeguard human rights in social programs is relatively idealized. In the real world, deviations of practice from
principle are seldom absent. Inequitable legislation and administrative
practices can and do arise in a system whose rules of procedure are themselves generally just. A large component of social progress consists in securing modifications to the procedural rules governing political decisions
in order to make them more just and more equitable. The rules for decision

115

making in social programs clearly are not ethically perfect. But on the whole, they do provide a reasonable set of guidelines in those situations where they are applicable.

To Whom May We Do Harm?

The central problem can be posed in terms of the ethical rules governing social decisions—in the form of programs or experiments—insofar as those decisions may have a significant possibility of harming some individuals or groups. Social experiments do not differ from social programs because the former may cause harm to some individuals and the latter not. Almost every decision about social policy, legislative or administrative, has a negative element—some people will, or at least may, be harmed.

There are two kinds of harm, absolute and relative. Some policies will result in directly reducing the welfare of some people, but the extent or nature of the harm cannot be gauged before programs go into action. It is not possible to guarantee that every child who goes into a Head Start program will suffer no harm. The Neighborhood Youth Corps, however desirable on balance, may in some cases promote poor work habits. And, very obviously, local school boards adopt new educational curricula that, while benefiting some children, harm others.

In other cases the harm is relative—persons in similar status receive quite unequal benefits. Most of the social programs adopted in recent years reach only a fraction of those eligible. The current low- and moderate-income housing subsidies are rationed; not all eligible families receive a subsidy. One family of four with a $5,000 income may get no subsidy while a neighboring family with a $6,000 income may have a housing subsidy worth $800 or $1,000 per year. Neighborhood health centers and community mental health clinics provide free or reduced-price care to a small fraction of the low-income urban population.

While some of these programs seem inequitable—certainly compared to an ideal situation—the procedural rules that govern them cannot be viewed as unethical simply because some actual or potential harm is created by a particular policy for some individuals. No social program is completely free of some probability of generating either absolute or relative harm.

Peter Brown lists the types of harms that might be visited on individuals or groups from social experiments.[1] Yet these same kinds of harm flow from legislative programs: The *direct risks or harms* that an experiment poses, such as a reduction in income or insurance benefits, are similar to the possible consequences of tariff policies or of changes in deductible costs and coinsurance in medical-care programs. The *induced risks or harms* that the social experiment may expose its subjects to—for example, health insurance provisions that induce doctors to provide less care—are evident in federal programs providing support of health maintenance organizations and in minimum wage laws that raise the cost of hiring secondary workers. The *risks of phaseout or termination* that may make the harmful effects exceed the benefits of an experiment are equally potent in defense contracts that build up a community and leave it depressed after termination, or in the Interstate Commerce Commission's revision of railroad rate schedules that have contributed to the development of a port. The *community risks or harms* that an experiment may induce through competition for a desired commodity, such as a general rent increase generated by a housing allowance experiment, may also arise from public policies that cause tight money and high interest rates, or from federal installations that benefit part of a community but raise rent for all.

Both social programs and social experiments carry with them the possibility of harm to some individuals. To what extent can the rules governing harm in the former be applied to the latter? How do various categories of social programs or policies relate to various categories of social experiments in their effect on individuals or groups? What rules for the protection of individual rights are used in legislating and executing social programs? Do the similarities and differences between social programs and social experiments dictate different protective rules and procedures for the two?

Categories of Social Policies and Experiments

When viewed in terms of potential harm, social programs or policies may affect individuals or communities in a number of different ways. Basically the same classifications may be used for social experiments.

1. See pp. 86–87, above.

Individual Consent

A very large number of social programs offer benefits or services that the individual is free to accept or reject. A mother is not required to send her child to a Head Start program; no one must take food stamps, enroll in a manpower training program, or use the medical services of a neighborhood health center. If harm occurs, it is an unintended side effect of a free choice on the part of the individual. In some cases misleading promises may have been made, but this is an aberration, not the working of the procedures themselves. Similarly in social experiments, individuals are offered certain benefits or services, and different groups are offered different packages. Individuals may accept or reject the offer.

Institutional Decision

Individuals may be affected by social policies that offer them little or no choice—for example, tariff policies, monetary regulations, and adoption of curricula in public schools. The policy changes the environment, and the individual must adapt. Some individuals are harmed in the process. In an experiment the subjects may be included on the basis of a choice made by an institution, such as a school board or a hospital. Three variations of such an experiment are possible: (1) The institution could have been offered a choice among a number of planned variations or have been assigned an experimental treatment; the institution would have elected to participate, but all individuals within the institution would have to be given the same experimental treatment. (2) An institution, either on its own initiative or through agreement with some other level of government, could apply different experimental treatments to individuals falling within its jurisdiction. (3) The institution may be required to participate in an experiment; a hospital, for example, may be required to take part in an experimental reimbursement scheme under Medicare.

Subsidies and Incentives

The federal government may offer subsidies to individuals, firms, or state and local governments to do something they would not otherwise have done. If investment tax credits or open-ended matching grants-in-aid should cause harm, it follows from a free choice by those affected— they miscalculated. But if the terms are fair and full information is provided, it is hard to aver inequity. Individuals may be compensated for joining an experiment, with the compensation designed to offset any disadvantages or to pay for inconveniences; for example, payments are offered to control groups, and compensation is promised to participants in a health insurance experiment. Individuals are free to accept or reject the offer.

Communitywide Effect

Whole communities may be affected by policy actions. The location of a defense establishment in a community may increase incomes for some and raise rents for others; termination of a military base may reverse this process. Changes in railroad regulations may harm some communities and greatly benefit others. Likewise, the result of an experiment may adversely affect communities as a whole, or significant portions of a community; a housing experiment, for instance, can induce rent increases.

In general, each of the ways in which individuals or groups may be affected in a social experiment has its analogue in social programs or social policies. But the rules of the game for adopting and executing social policies are not always adaptable to social experiments. What are the rules safeguarding individual rights in social policies? To what extent are these applicable or not applicable to social experiments, and what are the implications of the similarities and differences?

Rules for Regulating Harm

Social policies operate under the general presumption that, however great the uncertainty, legislators or administrators have chosen the policy that, among all the alternatives, appears the best. This does not mean the best on pure efficiency grounds. Rather it is the best choice, after taking into account all relevant factors, including the necessity of reconciling divergent views and interests. The presumption that the policy is the best choice may often be a fiction, but it is nevertheless a standard—inferior alternatives are not chosen deliberately.

It is the very nature of social experiments that this rule will not work. With a number of different treatments, the one facing a particular individual or group cannot be represented as a selection of the best. However great the uncertainty and ignorance of costs and benefits that surround the choice among alternatives in social programs, and however disputable the wisdom of a particular choice, those affected by it can presume that the policy stemmed from a process designed, in theory at least, to select the best socially acceptable alternative.

Some social programs, of course, offer services or benefits that the individual is not forced to accept. They are quite similar to social experiments that may be accepted or rejected. The difference is that the package of benefits offered in the social program was presumably selected as the best available package (however great the uncertainty surrounding the choice), whereas the package offered any one individual in the social experiment was not chosen as the best.

A second set of rules governing the choice of social programs stems from general recognition of a principle of increasing marginal harm (diminishing marginal utility with the sign reversed). The importance of avoiding harm to an individual grows more than proportionately with the degree of harm. As a consequence the legislative process appears to operate under a generally accepted, if somewhat imprecise, agreement that costs and benefits cannot simply be aggregated across a large number of individuals and a net balance struck. A single great harm to one individual (loss of life, deprivation of livelihood) is recognized to be more significant socially than the aggregation of small harms to a number of individuals. A procedural set of arrangements has grown up that gives specific political force to this recognition. In the real world of politics, lobbies, congressional committees, and pressure groups, the views and opinions of individuals and groups about a particular policy decision are given a weight that becomes larger the more seriously that decision directly affects them. Farmers and farm lobbies have a greater voice in the decisions of the Department of Agriculture and the agricultural committees than they do in the decision of the aeronautics and space committees. Educators carry greater weight with the executive and the Congress on matters of education than they do on oil depletion allowances.[2]

In the case of programs that offer individual services, a person in effect gets two votes: a weighted vote on the design of the package of benefits, and an absolute veto on his own participation—he can simply refuse to

---

2. Indeed, a substantial part of the recent attention to the rights of minorities and the poor has been devoted to a struggle to find ways of increasing the weight of their vote in matters that affect them. The weights actually assigned to various groups may not at any point in time be equitable. But the concept is essentially reasonable.

join. In the case of programs or policies that cannot be applied individually (tariff regulations, public school curricula, farm price support formulas, and so forth) the individual (more usually a group representing his interests) has only one weighted vote at the time the program or policy is designed.

The principle of increasing marginal harm, therefore, has two ethical consequences: one that offers a substantive criterion for policymaking—generally, when the costs of a program are judged, a very large harm to a few is not equated with a small harm to many, and a small probability of great harm is given great weight—and a second that affects procedures—votes in the game of political decision making are roughly weighted in proportion to the potential impact the decision can have on particular groups.[3]

Another aspect of the rules under which social programs are adopted is related to the time-honored practice of logrolling. Communities, regions, and groups have a chance to bargain, explicitly or implicitly, about packages of legislative or administrative decisions. Individual policies or actions that may cause harm to some groups can be balanced by other actions that provide benefits. A community or group can use its bargaining power to assure some balance in the total effect of social policies and programs on its interests. While the political and pressure group tactics used in the process are highly imperfect, and often cause program analysts to despair, they are a common method of securing some distributional balance of harms and benefits.

Application to Social Experiments

With a few exceptions, the current rules governing social experiments either coincide with the rules governing social programs where experiments and programs are similar, or provide adequate additional safeguards where the two situations are different.

Individual Consent

Social experiments that offer a package of benefits or services to individuals are only slightly different from social programs that offer such

3. The weighting of votes does not arise solely from the principle of increasing marginal harm. It is a means by which groups can assert their interest not only in avoiding large harms but also in any matter that bears particularly on their own welfare—be the effect positive or negative.

benefits or services. In both cases the individual consents to participate in the service or benefit. In both cases a positive effect on individual welfare is expected, but the possibility of harmful side effects cannot be ruled out. In both cases participants should be fully informed of the nature of the service and the conditions of participation. The amount of information needed in both experiments and programs depends on the particular case. (For example, a prospective recipient of a moderate-income home-owner-ship subsidy should be fully informed of the conditions of the mortgage and subsidy contract, which may incorporate a complicated set of terms.) In social programs the service or benefit offered has been chosen by a political process that, in theory at least, seeks the best socially acceptable alternative. In an experiment a number of different alternatives are being tested. Moreover, in social experiments the service is offered for a specific and limited period of time, while in social programs the time period depends on the legislative and administrative process—cutoff or cutback is possible. But these differences do not seem to warrant any special rules for experiments in this category beyond those now in existence.

Institutional Decision

There are variations of the social experiment that involve decisions by institutions or state governments rather than by individuals. In the planned variations and assigned treatments where the consent of the institution is secured, all individuals within the institution are subject to the same treatment. In this case, with one major exception, there seems to be no relevant difference between social programs and social experiments; the institution or the state or local government decides whether it wishes to accept a particular program or treatment. Whether the consent happens to be to a program or an experimental treatment is more or less irrelevant to the institution and those within it. Those responsible for policy decisions in the institution can calculate the desirability of consent and make their decisions with equal freedom in both cases.

The rules do not hold, however, if the institution, in the normal course of events, cannot be presumed to be representative of or acting in the interest of the individuals who are affected by the program or treatment. Normally, the federal government can presume that other governmental bodies—state and local governments, school boards, and the like—are acting on the basis of generally representative procedures. They are presumed to make decisions in the interests of those affected by the program or experimental treatment. While the representative process is subject to all sorts of imperfections, they are no more likely to exist in experiments than in governmental programs. Subject to strong contrary evidence, it seems reasonable for the federal government, in both situations, to assume the existence of a representative process.

Many nongovernmental institutions that might become the consenting agent for either programs or experiments cannot be presumed to represent the persons ultimately affected by the experiment. Private schools might participate in educational experiments; private mass transit companies might agree to become part of a mass transit experiment; hospitals might be asked to join an experiment dealing with shortened hospital stays or substitution of physicians' assistants on wards. When such institutions participate in generally applicable federal programs, the normal rules of political choice offer some assurance that various interests appropriately weighted have been represented in the choice process. The normal forms of political consent have been obtained.

There is no such assurance in the experimental situation. While the participating institutions will usually have reasons of self-interest to safeguard the rights of their clients who are affected, there is no guarantee that this will always be true. Hence special care and special rules may need to be applied: if the experiment affects an entire community (as does mass transit), approval from the relevant governing body should be sought; if private institutions (schools, hospitals) are involved, but no community-wide impact is expected, the approval of the relevant supervisory state or local institution (public health agency, state board of education) should be secured.

In experiments where the institution applies different treatments to different individuals within its jurisdiction the analogy to programs breaks down. No longer is the institution choosing a single treatment on behalf of those within the institution, and exercising judgment about the net value of that treatment. Insofar as any given treatment is concerned, no responsible and representative body is charged with agreeing to that treatment as a net benefit to the individuals receiving it. Hence consent of the institution to apply different treatments is not enough. The consent of the individuals concerned must be secured. This could be done through a vote of units within the institution (for example, the parents in each school within a school district). If such a vote is not feasible, consent of each subject individual may be required. Each program or experimental treatment must, according to this logic, receive the consent of either the experimental subject or of a body whose representative boundaries are coextensive with the individuals subjected to a treatment. Hence a school board may agree to accept a single treatment for those within its jurisdiction, but it cannot agree to apply a number of treatments. For each treatment a representative body must exist or be created in order to secure valid institutional consent.

Finally there is the sticky case of an experiment in which institutions are required to participate. Such an experiment is difficult but not impossible to conceive. Imagine an incentive reimbursement experiment for hospitals under Medicare and Medicaid. Voluntary participation could make the experiment meaningless, because of adverse selection.[4] Would such a required participation be ethical, and if so under what conditions? If all of the incentive reimbursement treatments would meet a standard of fairness and equity, so that conceivably any one of them could become national policy, and if the experimental treatment affected the institution and not the individuals served by the institution (a reimbursement experiment would meet this definition while a medical treatment experiment would not), then it seems to me that even mandatory experiments could be considered ethical.

Subsidies and Incentives

Social experiments that offer individuals compensation for participating in an experiment that may not itself provide net benefits are very analogous to federal subsidies offered to firms or individuals to induce them to change their behavior. The individual can decide whether the compensation is worth the costs to him of altering his behavior. The health insurance experiment is a case in point.

Two special caveats are in order here. First, program subsidies are most frequently designed for recipients who can be expected to calculate the trade-offs in a relatively sophisticated manner, either directly or with the aid of special-interest groups. Many experimental subjects may not be equally as capable of sophisticated calculation. Hence it is incumbent on the experimenter to explain the trade-offs fully, and not underplay any risks involved. Greater effort at laying out the costs and consequences should be expected in the case of experiments. Second, in cases where the

4. Technically, hospitals would not be legally required to join; they could choose to cease handling Medicare or Medicaid cases. But for all practical purposes, participation is effectively required if it is a condition for receiving Medicare or Medicaid reimbursement.

trade-off includes, as one component, a small probability of large harm (such as giving up catastrophic protection in a health insurance plan) some special rules may be necessary. It may be asking too much for those living on the edge of subsistence to judge in a balanced way the relative merits of an immediate monetary gain as against a very small probability of very large harm. While society generally proceeds on the assumption that even the poor and the disadvantaged are capable of entering into contracts and arrangements that may levy costs upon them, that freedom is sometimes restricted where large harm is possible—for example, in requiring seat belts (rather than allowing individuals to weigh the trade-off between the cost of optional belts and the avoidance of harm). Although social policy appears to be somewhat inconsistent in this regard, it seems desirable to eliminate small risks of great harm in experiments, rather than to offer compensation on an expected value (or a risk-adjusted value) basis.

Communitywide Effect

In experiments under which communitywide effects are anticipated, there seems to be no reason why approval by the relevant governing body would not meet all the requirements of safeguarding the rights of individuals. Many social policies and programs that have major impacts on communities, including harmful ones, are carried out without securing explicit agreements from the community (tariff charges, location of defense establishments, pollution control regulations, railroad rates regulations). There is a set of formal and informal procedures in the adoption and execution of such policies that works toward a rough balance of equity. These procedures are largely absent in the acceptance of experiments. But securing the consent of the local governing bodies—which gives them a veto—provides those safeguards in an even stronger form than is available in the case of social policy and programs. Again, while the resulting safeguards will not be perfect—since local governing bodies are not perfect—they are as strong if not stronger than the safeguards offered in many social policies or programs.

ALEXANDER MORGAN CAPRON

Social Experimentation
and the Law

Social reformers have always believed that means can
be found to improve the conditions of life and create better social institutions, but they have not always been systematic or scientific in testing
the reforms they were recommending. In recent years, however, they have
made increasing efforts to estimate in advance the costs and effects of
possible changes in social policies and institutions. One manifestation of
this trend has been the emergence of social policy experiments. These
attempts to gain more precise information about the effects of reforms
through systematic field trials of new policies and evaluation of results
are typified by the recent large-scale experiments on income maintenance,
housing allowances, health insurance, and education curricula. These
experiments involve some theoretical basis for predicting the expected
effects of new policies, intentional manipulation of policies to produce
information, and attempts to quantify policy effects. They are designed
and managed by social scientists, are undertaken on a large scale with
federal support, and consist mainly of studying the effect on individuals
and markets of changes in economic incentives and regulation.[1]

From the legal vantage point, social experimentation epitomizes the
central dilemma posed by all experimentation involving human beings:
when, in a society that values both knowledge and human dignity and
equality, may some people be used as means to serve the ends of the
group? Clearly, this issue is raised in many human activities. In most
types of experimentation it may be blunted, however. First, the mecha-

1. Systematic research on such social and legal institutions as the jury, which
would also seem to be "social experimentation," apparently has not been thought of
under such a rubric. Despite steps into the "real world," such research has generally
taken place in the laboratory under simulated conditions. See Harry Kalven, Jr.,
and Hans Zeisel, *The American Jury* (Little, Brown, 1966).

nisms for selecting subjects operate informally and with low visibility, and risks for subjects may be mitigated by the life-saving therapeutic benefits that they can derive from participating. And second, the potential returns accrue less to any identifiable group than to the body of scientific knowledge. In social experimentation, by contrast, these issues come immediately to the fore, since the choice of one subject over another is the result of a highly structured and quite visible process and is unrelated to the possibly greater needs of one person than another, and the beneficiary of the research is intended in a fairly specific and concrete sense to be the social collectivity, as embodied in governmental decision makers.

Social experimentation thus brings distributive justice into focus in a way that other instances of social regulation seem not to. Of course, each instance of rule formulation and invocation by lawmakers (lawyers, judges, and legislators), no less than each instance of patient treatment by physicians, is an "experiment," with potential effects not only for its immediate subjects but for all of society. Although those involved in the legal system are probably less aware than their medical colleagues of the experimental nature of almost everything they do, the element of uncertainty-of-outcome still enters into their decisions.

Recognition of the legitimate role of government in undertaking social and economic experiments has its roots in the Great Depression when the Supreme Court was faced with challenges to attempts by state and federal authorities to restore economic and social order. As Louis Brandeis observed in an eloquent dissent:

The discoveries in physical science, the triumphs in invention, attest the value of the process of trial and error. In large measure, these advances have been due to experimentation. In those fields experimentation has, for two centuries, been not only free but encouraged. Some people assert that our present plight is due, in part, to the limitations set by courts upon experimentation in the fields of social and economic science; and to the discouragement to which proposals for betterment there have been subjected otherwise. There must be power in the States and the Nation to remould, through experimentation, our economic practices and institutions to meet changing social and economic needs.[2]

Experimentation in Brandeis's day meant some untried departure from existing social or economic relationships. Since it lacked any theoretical framework or scientific controls, the significance of its results would be ambiguous at best. Nevertheless, the simple trial and error methods gained acceptance for massive, protracted, but unproven societal manip-

2. *New State Ice Co.* v. *Liebmann*, 285 U.S. 262, 310–11 (1932).

ulation; they thus paved the way for increasingly sophisticated attempts to control for extraneous influence so that the effects of reforms can be identified and measured. Current experimentation, which goes beyond "evaluation research" and influences the very design of the program being tested, is a more scientific offspring of these long-existing attempts by lawmakers to find means through which to alter society and the behavior of its members.

The enterprise of human experimentation generally has been the object of much criticism recently. Although the special nature of social experiments accentuates some problems now seen in all human studies, the increased use of social experiments would appear to be cause for cheer rather than dismay, because so much can be gained from carefully determining whether a proposed policy will achieve the results claimed for it before giving it full implementation. Furthermore, it may be misleading to analyze social policy research primarily under the heading of experimentation. Social experimentation departs from the natural experiments created by ordinary legislation more in the degree to which policy alternatives are consciously compared than in its effects on the interests of the various participants. This type of research must be viewed as much as a species of legislation as a species of experimentation. Hence, any guidelines, strictures, or prohibitions that are developed for social policy research may find application to other types of legislative experimentation, since it is difficult to draw lines that would distinguish among them.

Participants in the Experimental Process

Each of the participants in the social experimentation process—the investigator, the subject, the scholarly professions, and above all, the state —has a special set of interests in the process. The legal protections of those interests will be much like those that have developed around clinical research in the life sciences. Not only has the work of physicians, psychologists, and the life scientists led to the creation of a number of rules governing their research, but these groups have held the most prominent position as experts authorized to change people. Their experience seems pertinent in examining the problems raised by social experiments, the courts' methods in dealing with such problems, and the possibility that new rules or safeguards are needed in social policy experimentation. These rules will have to take into account the dual role of the state, which is not only the primary regulator, but, in the case of social experiments, also the sponsor and major beneficiary of the studies.

The law has many faces. It provides the means whereby social policy research is undertaken, distributes the burdens and benefits created thereby, restricts the scope of the participants' actions, and provides a means to resolve conflicts among them. The final role—that of mediator—is of particular interest in an area in which rules are not yet firmly drawn nor relationships well established. How can the law mediate conflicts between various interests: individual versus individual, group versus individual, and present versus future?

The Investigator

Social science investigators play a central role in the instigation, design, and execution of social experiments. A variety of personal and social forces are responsible for prompting an experiment in the social as well as the life sciences: individual curiosity, a professional consensus that the area is ready for study, public perception that a problem is badly in need of a solution, and the availability of research funds. The investigator is both catalyst and active agent in the process.

VALUES AND MOTIVATIONS. The social scientists in charge of policy experiments, like their medical counterparts in clinical experimentation, are motivated and guided by a number of value preferences, including drives toward independence, knowledge, and prestige. One such value is academic freedom, the scholar's right to pursue his research and writing without dictates from officials. The independence of the investigator is not unlimited, however, since his professional peers remain proper judges of the quality and persuasiveness of his work. Also, the social scientist is less of a free agent in experimentation than is his medical counterpart. For example, not merely in funding (where both social and medical scientists may find themselves beholden to the state) but in facilitation through legislative support (authority to select subjects, for instance), the state will play a more active role in social policy research.

The investigator's second value—the pursuit of knowledge—is closely linked to the first; indeed, it supplies the rationale for the first (that is, freedom and independence are needed to foster the pursuit of knowledge). The creation, as well as the communication, of ideas is an activity that is at the heart of the First Amendment. The Constitution appears to place no requirement of accuracy on the information that is developed or conveyed—although, of course, the law of libel and slander does create limits regarding information that concerns persons or groups, and high standards of accuracy or truth are part of the code of science itself.

The desire of the investigator not only to generate but to communicate new knowledge reflects a special scientific ethic. While the scientist loses control over his work by making it public, he also gains thereby in receiving the critical comments of his peers (which are needed to validate his work and to help him in carrying it further) and in establishing priority in the discovery or proof of his point. Thus, the norms of science—social, physical, and biomedical—make use of investigators' natural desire for prestige and acclaim to promote research and foster the other basic values of independence and knowledge.

METHODS OF INVESTIGATION. Once a social policy experimenter identifies problem areas, such as income transfer payments and medical insurance, in which he would like to investigate people's response to changes in government policy, what means will he choose to proceed?

The desire for independence and for accuracy of results may suggest that the investigator's first choice would be to operate fairly free of governmental involvement. Because he needs to study many subjects, however, he may find it useful to involve the government in the process of recruiting participants. In some cases the experimenter himself may have governmental power: as public defense attorneys had, for example, in studying the effects of various legal arrangements on the behavior of juveniles accused of crime,[3] and as a "juvenile-court judge of rather progressive and scientific mind" had in experimenting with variations in the place to which offenders were sentenced.[4] More frequently investigators enlist the aid of government officials who themselves have no particular expertise in experimentation.

An investigator, armed with governmental approval of his enterprise, might obtain subjects for his experiment either by having the government compel them to participate, or by recruiting volunteers himself. The mandatory participation of subjects has certain advantages to the investigator, especially if he is afraid that subjects' awareness of their participation in an experiment will change their behavior. For example, jury

3. Norman Lefstein, "Experimental Research in the Law—Ethical and Practical Considerations," in Jay Katz, with the assistance of Alexander Morgan Capron and Eleanor Swift Glass, *Experimentation with Human Beings* (New York: Russell Sage Foundation, 1972), pp. 333–36.
4. Paul A. Freund, "Ethical Problems in Human Experimentation," *New England Journal of Medicine*, vol. 273 (September 1965), p. 689.

deliberations in six civil cases in the federal district court in Wichita in 1954 were bugged by a group of lawyers and social scientists from the University of Chicago. Their research had been approved by the district judge and his superiors on the court of appeals and by the attorneys in each case, but the litigants and jurors (the latter being the primary subjects) were unaware that recordings were being made.[5] If the investigators had been required to use the alternative method of bargaining with potential subjects and, in effect, purchasing their cooperation, the experiment would not have been acceptable to either the researchers or the parties to the case.

For most social experimentation, it is likely that investigators will have to recruit paid or unpaid volunteers as subjects. This is generally the means employed for experimentation. Although the investigator will be able to maintain a good deal of control over the selection of subjects, since he sets the terms of the deal he is willing to offer, he faces more constraints than he would if participation were mandatory.

First, the cost of the experiment will be greater. In addition to bargaining with subjects, the investigator must persuade the government that public resources should be applied to his project rather than to other research or to other types of government programs. The more costly it is to obtain subjects, the more difficult will it be for him to get the government's support and cooperation.

Beyond this the investigator will be compelled to offer the potential subjects a sufficient inducement to obtain their cooperation. This not only compromises his independence to design the experiment entirely as he wishes but may also bias the selection of subjects toward a particular group or type of person who finds the inducement attractive. On the other hand, it may make the investigator more aware of costs, thereby eliminating unnecessary experiments and poor designs.

The Subject

The subjects of social policy experimentation will also have a set of values they wish to promote and protect. Briefly, they include privacy, self-determination, obtaining benefits and avoiding harm, and good governmental policy.

Personal privacy is, in many ways, the major bulwark against the manifold pressures of society. Many of the pressures—the increase of which

5. See Katz, *Experimentation with Human Beings*, pp. 67–109.

may account for the mounting interest in giving formal status to the concept of privacy—were created by scientific advances; yet it was "science that brought about the industrial revolution and made privacy physically possible."[6] The pressures come not only from the mechanical sciences but also from the social sciences, especially psychology.

While privacy has been a core concept of Western man for only a brief time, it seems undeniably to be a value that most people, not the least those who are the subjects of social experiments, desire to have respected. In this context, privacy refers both to areas of personality or conduct that an individual does not usually reveal to others except in limited ways and by permission (which relates to the value of self-determination), and to information revealed to one person—for example, a social policy experimenter—that may be deemed (implicitly or explicitly) for that person only and subject to release only in an anonymous or disguised form. Of course, the safeguarding of privacy may also be of interest to the investigator. The feeling of security that is fostered by the protection of privacy will increase both the willingness of subjects to confide and the probability that their behavior will be natural and not an artifact of being observed.

Another major interest of the research subject, given body in many legal rules, is in having authority to determine for himself what interactions he will engage in and what interferences with himself he will allow.

Belief in the idea of individual freedom is a cornerstone of the Western concept of man and society. The common law nurtures and protects individual freedom through the doctrine of self-determination, which confers on each person the right to pursue his own ends in his own way so long as he does not interfere with specified rights of other individuals or of the community. The requirement of consent is the primary means for implementing the abstract notion of self-determination. Tort law, for example, guards a man's property and person against interferences to which he has not consented. Similarly, a contract comes into being when two or more persons agree with each other that certain terms should govern their relationship.[7]

While man's increasingly interdependent existence seems to allow less scope for the operation of self-determination, it is a principle that has not been abandoned. Our rules of law serve not only to foster self-determination but to symbolize it as a primary value.

Subjects also, as rational economic beings, expect to receive benefit,

6. Oscar M. Ruebhausen and Orville G. Brim, Jr., "Privacy and Behavioral Research," *Columbia Law Review*, vol. 65 (November 1965), p. 1185.

7. Katz, *Experimentation with Human Beings*, p. 521.

and correlatively to avoid harm, from their participation in an experiment, be it financial, physical, or psychological. Finally, they may wish to promote good government, an aim that is both selfish and altruistic. Although this civic virtue—the interest a person has as a citizen (and perhaps as taxpayer) in promoting the general good—is part of the American ideology, it is given little concrete legal support and would have to be ranked at a lower level than the other values that guide subjects' conduct.

The Profession

Professional bodies help in the formulation of standards through the education and certification of future practitioners and the promulgation of codes of ethics. Professionals take part in the process of administering the rules and regulations established for human research, through participation in the peer review system for experimental protocols. (These mechanisms, established at the insistence of the federal government, still do not enjoy the full support of the professions.)[8] Both as a body and individually, professionals become involved in after-the-fact review of experimentation and its consequences, through such procedures as legislative hearings and lawsuits for damages.

The exercise of control by formal or informal groups of an investigator's professional colleagues has two major, and somewhat divergent, objectives. The primary concern has been to protect subjects, those too trusting and uncritical or too unsophisticated to detect experiments in which the risks outweigh the benefits. Since most human experimentation involves the helping professions, it is not surprising to find the paternalistic clinical practice that sets the client's best interests as a guide to the professional's decisions extended to the research setting. In recent years, professional oversight of the conduct of experiments has grown as the danger of improperly conducted experiments has become apparent within the professions. Not only may such experiments lead to a general lowering in professional standards for clinical practice, but they open the professions to censure by a public that perceives them as using human beings for guinea pigs.[9]

8. See, generally, Bernard Barber and others, *Research on Human Subjects: Problems of Social Control in Medical Experimentation* (New York: Russell Sage Foundation, 1973).

9. For an exploration of the reasons for ethical standards for researchers, see Henry Beecher, "Ethics and Clinical Research," *New England Journal of Medicine,* vol. 274 (June 1966), pp. 1354–60; Kai T. Erikson, "A Comment on Disguised Observation in Sociology," *Social Problems,* vol. 14 (1967), p. 366.

One of the most interesting features of social experimentation is that it involves social scientists for the first time in the practice of a profession in the sense that physicians practice theirs: interventions with individual patients. With the exception of psychologists, social scientists have applied their skills primarily in the construction of theories, for which the gathering and analysis of data (much of which relates, of course, to the activities of individuals) is a necessary and valuable adjunct; the practical side of such fields as economics and political science is largely exercised through participation in organizations that are concerned with manipulating institutions or with indirect means of influencing human behavior.

As the social science professions find their members involved in studies that place individuals at risk, they will have to consider whether they need ethical guidelines similar to those that the clinical professions adapted from their traditional norms; they will also have to decide whether it is possible to formulate standards for the proper execution of social experiments. Up until now, leaders in the social sciences have advocated more vigorous pursuit of social policy experimentation,[10] rather than sounding a cautionary note. While this attitude may be changing, it seems appropriate not to put any great emphasis on the professions as potential regulators. Certainly professional self-regulation of biomedical research has not been an altogether happy experience, and the very decision to treat an area as one appropriate for professional ethics suggests, erroneously, that the questions raised are within the competence of investigators to decide solely with guidance from their colleagues. Moreover, the major role that governmental bodies play in social policy experimentation probably means that they can best take the lead in regulating the process. If they are not sufficiently vigorous in protecting interests identified by the professions, the latter should promulgate the necessary additional protections.

The State

The objectives that lie behind state sponsorship of experimentation include increasing knowledge, achieving economy in government programs, and promoting dignity, liberty, and equality. The state's concern with knowledge is not premised solely on dedication to full and unfettered generation and dissemination of information, but also on the usefulness of data on the effects of legislation in decision making. Since such data

10. See, for example, Alice M. Rivlin, *Systematic Thinking for Social Action* (Brookings Institution, 1971).

are likely to be of limited, if any, economic value to others, social policy experiments will probably not be undertaken without state sponsorship.

Information gained through limited-scale experiments may help in formulating efficacious and economic social welfare programs. (The efficiency value should also affect the way experiments themselves are conducted.) Still, the data will only be of use in future decisions. No matter how efficiently an experiment is conducted, it cannot confidently be predicted to be of benefit to the subjects involved. Thus, the decision to permit social experiments, or all the more so to encourage and fund them, must be premised on a preference for future lives over present ones.

The pursuit of knowledge and economy, together with their inherent presumption in favor of future lives, tends to favor social policy experimentation. The promotion of three other basic values—dignity, liberty, and equality—may retard it. Dignity and liberty are fostered through the legal rules and institutions that assure the individual his right to self-determination; from this right proceeds each person's right to choose whether to participate in an experiment or to share private information with the researchers. The state values self-determination not only because it protects individual liberty and privacy but because the economic and political systems depend on people assuming responsibility for their choices. Only where individuals believe that their acts, including adverse consequences, are largely a result of their own decisions can a system of cooperation, with primary reliance on self-enforcement, be expected to succeed.

Finally, the principle of equality, to which the nation has a long-proclaimed albeit wavering attachment, must enter into the state's decision making about social experiments. As with liberty and dignity, adherence to equality as a value preference will place limits on the methods employed in research. Within these constraints, state sponsorship of social policy experiments is not inconsistent with allegiance to the values of self-determination and equality, although tensions will inevitably be present and in need of resolution.

Regulation of Experimentation

Governmental regulation of research with human beings has thus far been designed to protect experimental subjects through review of prospective research plans and retrospective evaluation of research that has resulted in harm. In the review of projected research, committees (until recently, made up largely of an investigator's institutional brethren) are asked to certify that a project's benefits outweigh its risks and that subjects' rights (including their right to informed consent) are protected.[11] After-the-fact review looks at whether the experiment was conducted without negligence and with proper consent of the subject. A set of rules on informed consent has grown up through these two mechanisms.

Informed Consent

The law has long been concerned with safeguarding individuals from harm caused by others. In the thirteenth century the criminal law against forcible injuries was extended to civil action for trespass. The interferences encompassed by the early law were so direct, severe, and even violent that the absence of consent could be assumed; as the scope of the action for trespass increased, the absence of consent became an element of the cause of action. Some offenses might be illegal if committed without consent, but permissible with it or if consent were implied from the context.

The rule that absence of consent is an element of an action for assault and battery applies in medical treatment, as elsewhere. Its classical statement was given by Judge Cardozo for the New York court of appeals: "Every human being of adult years and sound mind has a right to determine what shall be done with his own body; and a surgeon who performs an operation without his patient's consent commits an assault, for which he is liable in damages."[12]

Only in the last twenty years has that concept been elaborated, although the courts earlier considered claims that consent was invalid because it was coerced or fraudulently obtained. Beginning with the *Salgo*[13] case and then explicitly in *Natanson* v. *Kline,*[14] the attention of the judiciary focused on the level of the disclosure required to make a consent valid. The term used by the Kansas supreme court, *informed consent,* became the center of a hotly contested area of medical jurisprudence. The courts divided on

11. "Protection of Human Subjects," *Code of Federal Regulations,* title 45, pt. 46, secs. 46.1–46.22 (1974).

12. *Schloendorff* v. *New York Hospital,* 211 N.Y. 127, 129, 105 N.E. 92, 93 (1914).

13. *Salgo* v. *Leland Stanford, Etc. Bd. Trustees,* 154 Cal. App.2d 560, 317 P.2d 170 (1957).

14. 186 Kan. 393, 350 P.2d 1093 (1960), clarified and rehearing denied, 187 Kan. 186, 354 P.2d 670 (1960).

the legal theory on which informed consent should be based; some simply ignored the niceties and merged the theories. "A physician may now be held liable either for negligence in a malpractice suit, if he breaches his duty to inform a patient, or for battery, if his failure to inform is found to have vitiated the patient's consent."[15]

Recently several courts have further narrowed the scope of the physician's discretion, holding that he is liable when the patient proves that a reasonable person would want the information that the physician withheld, without having to show that the physician deviated from any standard of medical practice.[16] The requirement of full disclosure to allow the patient to exercise his free will voluntarily and knowingly is set by law, except where an emergency exists or where the patient is incompetent.

While there is every reason to think that the requirement of informed consent would apply with as much, if not more, force in experimentation as in therapy, the application of the rule to experimentation has come about largely outside the courts; indeed, cases involving medical research seldom seem to reach appellate decision. The handful of eighteenth and nineteenth century cases on medical experimentation involved the application of new treatments to individual patients without a controlled or well-prepared experimental plan.[17] The concept of negligence was then in its infancy. While these early cases recognize that innovation is necessary or "all progress in the practice of surgery or physic must cease," still "the surgeon who does it [must be] prepared to take the risk of establishing, by his success, the propriety and safety of his experiment."[18]

Gradually the courts moved toward the negligence theory that was coming to prevail in all cases of medical treatment. For example, in *Jackson* v. *Burnham* the Colorado supreme court reiterated the accepted rule that "if a physician sees fit to experiment with some mode [besides the one upheld by consensus in the profession], he should do so at his peril," but then went on to suggest that a good defense would be proof that "he had reason for the faith that was in him," and that "his experiment [was justified] by some reasonable theory."[19]

15. Katz, *Experimentation with Human Beings*, p. 523.

16. *Cobbs* v. *Grant*, 104 Cal. Rptr. 505, 502 P.2d 1 (Sup. Ct. 1972); *Wilkinson* v. *Vesey*, 295 A.2d 676 (R.I. 1972); *Canterbury* v. *Spence*, 464 F.2d 772 (D.C. Cir. 1972), certiorari denied, 409 U.S. 1064 (1972).

17. The cases appear in Katz, *Experimentation with Human Beings*, pp. 526–29.

18. *Carpenter* v. *Blake*, 60 Barb. 488 (N.Y. Sup. Ct. 1871), reversed on other grounds, 50 N.Y. 696 (1872).

19. *Jackson* v. *Burnham*, 20 Colo. 532, 39 Pac. 577, 580 (1895).

In the leading modern judicial opinion on human experimentation, *Halushka* v. *University of Saskatchewan,* the Canadian judges extended the requirements of disclosure and agreement from the therapeutic to the research setting:

There can be no exceptions to the ordinary requirements of disclosure in the case of research as there may well be in ordinary medical practice. . . . The subject of medical experimentation is entitled to a full and frank disclosure of all the facts, probabilities and opinions which a reasonable man might be expected to consider before giving his consent.[20]

The holding in *Halushka* was partly responsible for inclusion of informed consent as a requirement in the initial guidelines on government-supported medical experimentation promulgated in 1966. Other influences were the ethical codes of professional bodies such as the World Medical Association's Declaration of Helsinki, the attention focused by Dr. Henry Beecher on unethical medical experiments being conducted at the time, and the first principle in the Nuremberg judgment on the Nazi prison camp physicians ("The voluntary consent of the human subject is absolutely essential"),[21] which was in itself an extraordinary example of common law decision making. The federal guidelines have since been greatly elaborated, but the commitment to the principle that the investigator must obtain subjects' voluntary consent after a "full and frank disclosure" of relevant information has not wavered. It has now been given judicial recognition in the unusual context of a suit brought to halt a proposed experiment, rather than to seek compensation for injuries suffered in a completed one.[22]

A corollary to the respect that informed consent gives to individual autonomy is the responsibility that it places on each individual for the consequences of his own free choices. The research subject's major obligation will be to comply with the good faith requests of the investigator on matters coming within the scope of the undertaking. It is often stated that subjects must be given the unconditional right to withdraw from an experiment at any time. Though this rule is obviously necessary in medical research (principally to avoid overreaching by the investigator in the case

20. 52 W.W.R. 608, 616–17 (Sask. 1965).

21. Nuremberg Code, reprinted in Katz, *Experimentation with Human Beings,* pp. 305–06.

22. *Kaimowitz* v. *Michigan Department of Mental Health,* Civil Action No. 73-19434-AW (Cir. Ct., Wayne Co., Mich., July 10, 1973), holding that involuntarily detained mental patients could not undergo experimental psychosurgery because their competency, knowledge, and voluntariness (elements of informed consent) could not be reliably ascertained.

of painful and perhaps even life-threatening research), it seems questionable whether it should be taken over whole into the social policy area. While the subject should not be forced to perform his contract if he wishes to cancel it, it may be appropriate to include a provision for liquidated damages should the subject withdraw without adequate reasons, spelled out in advance, which reflect the nature of the risks and inconveniences involved in the research. This should not be made so burdensome, however, that poor subjects will be precluded from exercising their choice; setting aside a small part of the compensation in escrow until the project is completed should be a fair compromise.

Protection of Confidential Information

The protection of confidentiality is one of the major issues raised by social experimentation, even though data collected in experiments is intended to be released only in a form of aggregated statistics. Information made public in this manner would appear to be harmless for individual subjects, but possibly detrimental for the subjects as a whole if they are identifiable as a social, economic, racial, or ethnic group. If information held by the investigators on individual subjects is disclosed to third persons, the subjects may suffer considerable embarrassment, discomfort, or inconvenience.

Confidentiality, as used by the law, refers to the duty that certain persons (typically, professionals) have not to reveal information that they have received in the course of their practice; they are liable for a breach of their responsibility to protect these confidences. This aspect of privacy could be (and apparently has been) handled adequately in social experiments, by expressing such a responsibility as part of the contract between investigator and subject, just as in contracts between physician and patient or attorney and client it is either expressly agreed to or, more often, required by the common law or by professional licensing statutes.

A contract solely between investigator and subject cannot adequately preclude disclosure that is compelled by third parties, particularly the state. This presents an issue that is related to that of confidentiality: whether there is a legal privilege to resist forced disclosure of information conveyed under a promise of secrecy. In the attorney-client relationship, the concept of a testimonial privilege is very old. But the privileges to withhold information gained by physician or psychotherapist from patient, accountant from client, priest from penitent, journalist from source are conferred by the legislature.

If, as social researchers believe, it is "essential to the value of the social experiment that the answers be as accurate as possible, and that biases and inaccuracies be identified in order to correct for them,"[23] an assurance of privileged communication may be needed. When researchers probe for accurate data they are likely to turn up information—concerning, for instance, living arrangements among people not related by law and perhaps not known to welfare officials, or sources of income that are either illegal or have been concealed from welfare or revenue officers—that subjects would be reluctant to make public but that law enforcement officials would be eager to discover. If, as seems to be the case, at least some social policy experiments are important enough to be given the benefit of a privilege, three routes are possible. All are premised to some extent on the state's placing greater weight on the benefits it will obtain from the experiment than on its interest in seeing the laws enforced, when the latter would cause it to violate the confidences of researcher and subject.

The first would be statutory protection for information revealed to investigators as part of a social policy experiment, like the confidentiality given census data that is directly in the hands of the government itself.[24] The task here is to define the limits of the statutory privilege: how necessary, if at all, must the information be to the experiment, and is the privilege waived, as has traditionally been the case, when the information is also revealed by the subject to third parties?

The second would be to develop the constitutional roots of privileges, in freedom of expression, right to privacy, and the rights of criminal defendants; some have argued that the testimony of subject to researcher be recognized as privileged on such grounds.[25] Courts have, however, recently rejected this line of reasoning when it was asserted by journalists

23. David N. Kershaw and Joseph C. Small, "Data Confidentiality and Privacy: Lessons from the New Jersey Negative Income Tax Experiment," *Public Policy*, vol. 20 (Spring 1972), p. 258.

24. Beyond census, and some health data, there are few statutory protections for confidentiality of data in governmental hands. The Comprehensive Drug Abuse Prevention and Control Act of 1970 authorizes the secretary of HEW, and the attorney general, to give researchers the authority to protect their subjects' anonymity, and they "may not be compelled in any Federal, State, or local civil, criminal, administrative, legislative, or other proceedings to identify such individuals." *United States Code*, title 42, sec. 242(a) (1970 ed.).

25. See Paul Nejelski and Lindsey Miller Lerman, "A Researcher-Subject Testimonial Privilege: What to Do before the Subpoena Arrives," *Wisconsin Law Review*, vol. 1971, no. 4, pp. 1085–1148.

and scholars who sought judicial recognition of privileges against having to testify about their sources of information.[26]

A third route would depend on the willingness of a responsible official to make a promise of privilege in advance. Suppose that prior to enrolling in the income maintenance experiments, the subjects had been assured by the local prosecutor that nothing they revealed to the people conducting the experiment would be used against them in court. Assume further that the prosecutor later became convinced that the social scientists had uncovered evidence of welfare fraud and he called them to testify before a grand jury. If the welfare recipients should refuse to give the information (based on their Fifth Amendment right not to incriminate themselves), do the experimenters have the right to assert a privilege has been created that protects their subjects? Under statutory authority, witnesses may be given immunity "in the public interest" by a judge or prosecutor to compel them to answer questions that could otherwise be declined on Fifth Amendment grounds. Thus, the question is reduced to whether a proper basis exists by analogy to say that where information is "compelled" by the promise that it will not be used, the promise is binding when a formal immunity statute does not apply.

The interests in the two situations are similar, and so-called use immunity (which would be involved here) enjoys constitutional status as being coextensive with the privilege against self-incrimination.[27] Ordinarily, witnesses are granted immunity from prosecution in exchange for information for an investigation, while here they would be seeking immunity from questioning in an investigation. Yet this extension is logical, since the purpose of questioning the researcher is to get information with which to prosecute the subject; if the subject cannot be prosecuted on the basis of the information that he supplied, then it would seem improper to compel the researcher to provide this information. Thus the information would be deemed privileged in order to preserve the subject's immunity.

If the prosecuting official who strikes the bargain has jurisdiction over the crimes that would be covered by the information collected from the subjects, he is at least arguably the proper person to grant immunity. It is within his discretion whether to prosecute,[28] although his jurisdiction

26. *Branzburg* v. *Hayes,* 408 U.S. 665 (1972); *Popkin* v. *United States,* 460 F.2d 328 (1st Cir. 1972).

27. *Kastigar* v. *United States,* 406 U.S. 441 (1972).

28. See, for example, *Inmates of Attica Correctional Facility* v. *Rockefeller,* 477 F.2d 375 (2d Cir. 1973); *Powell* v. *Katzenbach,* 359 F.2d 234 (D.C. Cir. 1965), certiorari denied, 384 U.S. 906 (1966), rehearing denied, 384 U.S. 967 (1966).

over the question is much more tenuous than when a crime has already been committed. Yet present Fifth Amendment case law would bar not merely the individual prosecutor but his successors or colleagues in other jurisdictions[29] from seeking to compel testimony from the investigators on matters protected by this privilege.

Government as Investigator

What effect should the government's being the investigator have on the applicability of regulations governing informed consent? It might be argued that, since the state is much more deeply involved in social policy experimentation than in the experiments for which the regulations were developed, the need for such regulations is greatly reduced. The government is far more interested in social experiments than in biomedical research, since the object of the studies is a governmental program, not a naturally occurring disease, and since the experiment may be undertaken under legislative aegis. Nevertheless, it would seem that "in so far as the government itself participates in the system"[30] it should be held to the same requirements, for the same reasons, as independent investigators. Indeed, there are good reasons to create a higher standard for consent when the intervention is at the prompting of the state rather than a private party. A reflex response of unthinking cooperation with official inquiries may make some people less self-protective. Furthermore, our constitutional scheme is replete with indications (such as the Fourth Amendment) that governmental actions affecting privacy are to be closely confined.

On balance, it seems to me that social experiments in which the government is involved ought to be conducted under the same regulations as have been developed for other human research. There may be circumstances, however, in which it is appropriate and permissible for the state to bypass the rules on consent and require participation, on the basis of the "consent of the governed" rationale which lies behind all legislation. This rationale is also helpful in analyzing the problems created by the substantial ripple effects of social policy experiments. Unless the people af-

---

29. *Murphy* v. *Waterfront Commission,* 378 U.S. 52 (1964), holds that a witness in a state proceeding is protected by the privilege against self-incrimination under federal law, and vice versa; *Santobello* v. *New York,* 404 U.S. 257 (1971), holds that failure of prosecution to keep promise regarding recommendation of sentence is ground for withdrawing guilty plea.

30. Thomas I. Emerson, "Toward a General Theory of the First Amendment," *Yale Law Journal,* vol. 72 (April 1963), p. 895.

fected by such ripples are classified in a somewhat different way than as subjects of social experiments, their informed consent will have to be sought.

Clearly, there are degrees of being a subject. For example, a study of the effects on behavior of welfare legislation could be conducted by simply collecting information that is publicly available. Although such data might permit the social scientists to suggest the effects of "naturally occurring" variations in such legislation and regulations, there would be no manipulation of the population for study purposes, and these persons would not need to be treated as subjects. It is, nevertheless, possible that some of the concerns that lie behind the requirement of consent would arise here; most particularly, the compilation of data from a number of sources might lead to breaches in confidentiality not inherent in the separate uses for which the data were originally gathered. Policy considerations would thus argue that steps be taken to preserve anonymity, but it would not seem necessary to seek consent from such persons, unless the use of the information about them goes beyond that which they were implicitly or explicitly led to expect when it was collected. In sum, such persons, though the objects of study, come close to being nonsubjects.

A different case is presented by those who are indirectly affected by the manipulations of social experimenters; while the experimenters may not be seeking data about this group of people, they are having some measurable impact on their lives. The first issue in regulating such experiments is to determine which effects are significant enough to categorize a person as a remote subject rather than as a nonsubject.

There are also problems, both logistical and scientific, in any attempt to treat a group of remote subjects like subjects. How will the remote subjects actually be identified, contacted, compensated, educated, and "signed on" for the experiment? The biasing effects on behavior brought about by subjects' knowledge that they are participating in an experiment can only be worsened if additional people are made aware of the artificial, and perhaps temporary, nature of their condition. For example, if landlords (who are remote subjects in housing allowance and income maintenance experiments) are repeatedly told that the pressure for more and better accommodations is only a passing consequence of a government experiment, their responses to the market incentives are that much less likely to reflect their actual future behavior accurately.

There is finally the question of whether consent of the remote subjects is unnecessary on the ground that the experiment should be treated as an ordinary and proper function of government. A remote subject probably experiences alterations in his financial and social position that hardly differ from those caused by nonexperimental programs conducted by the government, or by myriad other influences on his life. In terms of risk, then, and because the remote subject is not an object of direct interest or inquiry, there would seem to be no reason to have to seek his consent. Still, the forces to which he is being subjected are not the result of ordinary legislation. In a democracy his specific consent may not be needed for the ways in which his interests are impaired or promoted by governmental actions, because he consents to that as part of the process of government, in which he participates. But should this rationale be used in the case of social experimentation?

Wide as the notion of the consent of the governed sweeps, it does not serve as a cover for legislative or executive action that is unconstitutional. At base, a democratic legal system is one in which each person participates and, optimally, concurs in each decision taken by the collectivity; majority rule and representation (rather than direct participation) attenuate the notion of participatory agreement somewhat, but do not alter it fundamentally. Yet in describing the scope of legislative power, constitutions unfortunately speak in terms that are either very narrow and precise or extremely general. Social policy research is not prohibited, but neither was it contemplated by the framers of the U.S. Constitution and, in treating groups of people differently and digging into details of their private lives, it may depart from the letter and spirit of the framers' great charter.

Any conclusion on whether legislatures have the power to experiment seems a very thin reed on which to place the decision whether consent need be sought from the remote subject of a social experiment. Moreover, another rule of constitutional adjudication that bears on the presumed legitimacy of government actions holds that a citizen cannot challenge a governmental decision simply because he disagrees with it. Rather, he has "standing" to bring an action pleading that a law is invalid only when he is personally adversely affected in an economic, physical, or aesthetic sense.[31] Consequently, even were a person to believe that a social experiment exceeded the powers that citizens have given their representatives and to the exercise of which they impliedly consent, he would still have to show that the governmental action had subjected him to greater burdens

31. *Sierra Club* v. *Morton*, 405 U.S. 727 (1972); *Data Processing Service* v. *Camp*, 397 U.S. 150 (1970); *Hardin* v. *Kentucky Utilities Co.*, 390 U.S. 1, 7 (1968); *Chicago* v. *Atchison, T.&S.F.R. Co.*, 357 U.S. 77 (1958).

or dangers than would otherwise be the case. Thus the question of risk, and the degree of cooperation needed from the remote subject by the social experimenters, will determine whether consent must be obtained from remote subjects in the case of experiments conducted by the government as in private ones, even when the rationale for action is the consent of the governed.

Liability for Damages

When should damages be charged against experimenters (and their sponsors)? This reflects a further complication of the problem raised by all experimentation. Assuming that experiments are usually conducted by persons practicing a profession, the experimenter would be held liable for malpractice if he breached the standards of conduct of his profession. It is difficult to follow this standard closely, however, since an experiment is, by definition, a departure from accepted customs in the profession. Either all experimenters must be held liable since they all break the rules (an unacceptable holding, at least since the mid-nineteenth century) or each component of each experiment must be judged separately for its conformance to custom. But such a procedure evades the real question of whether it was proper to put all the components together in some novel fashion. In some circumstances, it may even be argued that the risks created by an experiment are so great that any resulting harm should be governed by the principles of strict liability rather than negligence. This may also seem desirable if it appears that the experimenters are in a good position to minimize the injuries, and that it would be preferable (for economic reasons or for reasons of fairness) not to allow catastrophic injuries to befall any one individual as a consequence of his having been an experimental subject.

The issue of liability is complicated in social experimentation because such research is conducted by social scientists who do not possess the articulated norms of clinical practice that typically exist for persons engaged in biomedical experiments. It would thus be even harder to determine whether a social policy experimenter had behaved negligently in designing or executing a project.

Another major question about awarding damages to participants in social policy experiments concerns measurement of the damages. Subjects may suffer injury not only when an experimental protocol is violated (for example, by a breach of confidentiality) but also as a direct and intended result of an experiment (the tastes of participants in a negative income tax experiment, for example, may be so altered that they can no longer be satisfied if they do not possess certain goods that they cannot afford once the experiment ends). Yet even accepting the possibility of damage, how are damages of a noneconomic sort to be measured? From what point are they to be measured—the position the subjects were in at the beginning of the experiment, the position they would have been in at the point in time when the experiment ended had the experiment not been conducted, the position they would have been in had the experiment been conducted but had they not been its subjects, or the position that they are shortly to be in as a result of legislative action (advantageous or disadvantageous to persons in their category) that is premised on the results of the experiment? None of the first three is entirely satisfactory but each is at least an arguably valid basis for measurement. The fourth might best be regarded as ground for mitigation of any damages found to have occurred; to allow it to enter the calculations, however, raises a question of distributive justice because it would reduce the damages awarded to a subject on the grounds of the benefits he is receiving as a member of a class of people many of whom were not exposed to comparable burdens.

Mandatory Participation in Experiments

For both scientific and practical reasons, social science investigators and the state (and even some subjects) prefer to avoid bargaining as a means of obtaining experimental subjects. It is thus not surprising to discover that compulsory participation in social experiments has already occurred. In such experiments the government typically will not only lend its coercive authority in selecting a group of subjects but will also play an active supervisory role. In many cases the experiment will be a modified version of an existing governmental program. Compulsory participation raises many issues related to state sponsorship; the most fundamental problem is the unequal distribution of risks and burdens that occurs when selected individuals become the involuntary subjects of research intended to benefit a larger group or society as a whole.

Court Rulings on Social Experiments

Participants in at least two social experiments have gone to court to challenge the legality of the projects, one of which involved medical care benefits in California and the other work relief benefits in New York. Although these experiments were upheld primarily on statutory grounds, the courts' rulings indicate how both statutory and constitutional law apply in compulsory experimentation.

In California, recipients under the state's federally funded medical care program "paid nothing for any of the covered services or prescription drugs."[32] The state set up an experiment to see whether charging recipients one dollar for each visit to a health professional and fifty cents on each prescription (to a maximum total of three dollars per month) would reduce the utilization of health services, and hence the cost of the program, without adversely affecting their health status. In this "copayment" experiment, recipients who were not receiving cash under a federally funded "categorial aid" program and all "categorial aid" recipients who either had additional income or had possessions valued above certain prescribed levels were required to make the prescribed payments.

A number of recipients who had been placed in the experiment, as well as organizations such as the California Welfare Rights Organization to which they belonged, brought action against the secretary of health, education, and welfare. They contended that he had exceeded his authority to conduct demonstration projects, which was limited to those deviations which "in the judgment of the Secretary [are] likely to assist in promoting the objectives" of a particular section of the Social Security Act.[33] The medical care section specifies that "any deduction, cost sharing, or similar charge imposed under the plan" must be "reasonably related . . . to the recipient's income or his income and resources."[34] Since none of the recipients was able to pay anything for medical care, "the amount of payment that could be required as reasonably related to income and resources [was] precisely zero," as the federal court concluded.[35] Therefore, the plaintiffs argued, an experiment that charged fees for people who were unable to pay did not promote, but rather departed from, the objectives of the program.

The court ruled for the defendants on this question. The judge concluded that the experiment was consistent with the overall objectives of the program, including that of broadening the available medical services

32. *California Welfare Rights Organization* v. *Richardson,* 348 F.Supp. 491, 494 (N.D. Cal. 1972).

33. *United States Code,* title 42, sec. 1315.

34. Ibid., sec. 1396(a)(14)(B).

35. *California Welfare Rights Organization* v. *Richardson,* 348 F.Supp. 491, 495 (N.D. Cal. 1972).

to a comprehensive program by 1977. Indeed, he noted, the copayment project might point to the only way in which it may "be fiscally possible to achieve such comprehensive coverage."[36]

The California case thus seems to establish the acceptability of a social policy experiment run under an existing program if the experiment is intended to yield results that will improve the design of the program. The requirement that any experiment approved by the secretary under his authority to conduct demonstration projects must be submitted to Congress[37] provides a safeguard against executive amendment of a statute in a manner inconsistent with the legislative will. The case also illustrates the wide range of discretion permitted to governmental bodies in designing social policy experiments and the reluctance of judicial officers to rule on the wisdom or efficacy of such experiments.

These conclusions are confirmed by the litigation over the "work relief" experiments in New York.[38] In two experimental work programs for employable persons the subject pool was drawn along geographic lines, to encompass 25 percent of the families receiving aid to families with dependent children (AFDC) in the state.

In the major experiment, AFDC recipients who were found to be employable, but who lacked regular employment or training, were registered with the state employment service. If the service was unable to place a person in a private sector job within thirty days, he was assigned to a job with a state or local agency. The number of hours to be worked was based on his AFDC grant so that, in effect, the welfare recipient would earn all or a large part of his benefits. For those who failed to cooperate with the program, AFDC assistance was terminated.

The second experiment involved a group of these workers whose terms of employment were modified in four respects. First, they could be assigned to full-time jobs under the federal Emergency Employment Act, even if their compensation would exceed their AFDC grants; moreover, they could accept all fringe benefits usually attaching to such jobs. Second, a certain portion of the wages they were paid was to be ignored in determining the level of their AFDC grants. Third, school children over fifteen years old in subject families were required to participate in a work program after school and during the summer. Fourth, those who did

36. Ibid., 497.
37. *United States Code,* title 42, sec. 1320.
38. *Aguayo* v. *Richardson,* 473 F.2d 1090 (2d Cir. 1973).

not comply with the terms of the experiment were to have their AFDC assistance reduced by $66 per month.

The New York experiments clearly raise the question of equal protection, since two special classes were created, on a geographic basis, to provide a small population for test purposes. They also illustrate the use of a social experiment to achieve results that would have been impossible under the existing federal statute. When the New York work rules were first adopted in 1971, they were found by HEW to be inconsistent with federal requirements. They were subsequently approved as an experiment. Aguayo and the other New York plaintiffs objected, as those in the California case had, that the work experiments would not "assist in promoting the objectives" of the Social Security Act and thus could not be conducted. Chief Judge Friendly, disposing quickly of this argument, found that the federal welfare programs were intended to help recipients "attain or retain capability for the maximum self-support and personal independence," and that plaintiffs' objections that it was improper to force recipients to work were "clearly misdirected." The court also concluded that the power of the secretary of health, education, and welfare to waive requirements was broad enough to permit an alteration in the eligibility requirements and not merely in administrative techniques.[39]

The plaintiffs had contended further that, even if the goals of the experiments were consistent with the Social Security Act, the experiments "simply cannot in fact achieve the objectives or any of them." In addition to complaining about coercive and unfair aspects of the programs, the plaintiffs argued that it was unlikely that experience gained in the programs would qualify recipients for employment in the general economy, or even that comparable jobs would be available. The *Aguayo* court suggested that these arguments "were to some extent contradictory" of plaintiffs' basic contention that the experiments would have adverse effects on a great many welfare recipients. Moreover, resolution of this issue was the point of conducting the experiments. "Ascertainment by actual demonstration whether the latter claim is true would itself be a legitimate objective."[40] Thus, the production of knowledge about the factors underlying legislative choices on what social policies to pursue is held to be an inherent part of the purpose of all social policy legislation.

39. Ibid., 1103–05.
40. Ibid., 1105–06.

The court went even beyond this sweeping support for experimentation, generally following the guidelines established earlier for the judicial review of administrative actions in the absence of an adversary hearing, record, or statement of reasons. Those guidelines direct judges to determine "whether the decision was based on a consideration of the relevant factors and whether there has been a clear error of judgment."[41] The *Aguayo* court suggests that judges should be more lenient in reviewing the decision to conduct a social experiment than they would otherwise be:

We find more merit than do the plaintiffs in the defendants' position that, purely legal issues apart, it is legitimate for an administrator to set a lower threshold for persuasion when he is asked to approve a program that is avowedly experimental and has a fixed termination date than a proposal, like that in *Overton Park,* which is irreversible.[42]

In concluding that Secretary Richardson had made no "clear error of judgment," the court reasoned that the "relevant factors" for the secretary's consideration included "the fact that the programs were of limited duration and would remain under the on-going supervision (with the power to terminate approval) of HEW."[43]

The court may have been suggesting in the New York case that the very uncertainty that makes an experiment necessary also justifies engaging in the experiment. By such a reading, congressional authorization of experimentation with social security programs becomes a limitless authorization to engage in research in any area of social policy in which definitive answers cannot be given to such questions as "Can this program be improved?" or "What makes people in this program act as they do?" This interpretation is reinforced by the *Aguayo* court's observation that "experience will be the best test of . . . [the plaintiffs'] fears." The court thus concluded that "a strong showing" of the predicted adverse results of the experiment would have to be made by the plaintiffs "to demonstrate that the Secretary could not properly subject them to it."[44]

An alternative—and much narrower—reading of the ruling in *Aguayo* would hinge on the "avowedly experimental"[45] nature of the programs. This interpretation would seem to admit that the secretary may make mistakes but that they will be "of limited duration" and not "irreversible." But the difficulty with this reading of the decision is that the *Aguayo*

41. *Citizens to Preserve Overton Park* v. *Volpe,* 401 U.S. 402, 416 (1971).
42. *Aguayo* v. *Richardson,* 473 F.2d 1090, 1103 (2d Cir. 1973).
43. Ibid., 1106.
44. Ibid.
45. Ibid., 1103.

standard would encompass nearly all social legislation or programs carried out by administrators, which can all be viewed as experimental and terminated if they proved deleterious.

In sum, the New York decision further supports the inference of the California decision that, once Congress permits experimentation, the persons charged with program administration have broad, indeed nearly unreviewable, discretion in deciding when and how to conduct the experiments.

Constitutional Issues in Mandatory Experiments

The rational basis and the limits of social experiments have constitutional as well as statutory dimensions. Both the due process clause of the Fifth and Fourteenth Amendments and the equal protection clause of the Fourteenth impose major potential limitations on social experimentation.

PROBLEMS OF MEANS. Over the past thirty-five years the judiciary has avoided "substantive due process" analysis under which it had earlier passed on the permissibility of the ends that the legislature seeks to promote. Recently, however, a greater willingness has emerged to scrutinize governmental action to determine its "substantial relationship" to legislative ends.

Thus, if the state were to argue that it has a legitimate interest in new and useful knowledge in a particular area, a court reviewing the action of the legislature or executive might be called upon to decide whether the means adopted were appropriate to meet this goal. In *Aguayo*, Judge Friendly held that the state's legitimate desire "to determine whether and how improvements can be made in the welfare system" is " 'suitably furthered' by controlled experiment, a method long used in medical science which has its application in the social sciences as well."[46] Yet the opinion gives no hint that the district judge had received any evidence on how the experiment was conducted—whether any control group was established, for instance. Proof of the experiment's scientific validity would seem to be a minimum requirement if due process is to play any part in deciding about social policy experiments.

Just how scrutiny is to be undertaken is another question. It can certainly not be by a mere recitation of formulas about "rational relationships" and "substantial furtherance," but neither can it be by judicial weighing of the propriety of the means being used in social experiments.

46. Ibid., 1109.

Judges (as well as legislators and administrators) can be expected, however, to satisfy themselves that the burdens on the public fisc and on the lives of the subjects are justified by well-designed and properly executed research. It would seem appropriate for them to rely on social scientists not connected with the experiment in question to criticize it and to affirm or deny its basic soundness. Although courts in malpractice cases rely on physicians and other professionals to set the standards for practice in their fields,[47] a better system for technical advice on social experiments would be to rely on the decisions reached by review committees established under the HEW guidelines on protection of human subjects.

It is unlikely that most of the economically oriented social experiments now being conducted would trigger close judicial scrutiny because they do not potentially deprive their subjects of any interest that has been found to be fundamental. In addition to some rights explicitly recognized in the first ten amendments, such as freedom of press and of speech, the "list of interests identified as fundamental by the Warren Court was in fact quite modest: voting, criminal appeals and the right of interstate travel were the prime examples."[48] Indeed, the school, welfare, and housing experiments involve matters that the Supreme Court has explicitly held not to be fundamental.[49]

The one fundamental interest—privacy—that is likely to be infringed by social investigators remains ill-defined. It is certainly in the individual's interest to keep uninvited agents of the state out of the area over which he exercises control and in which he reasonably may expect not to be disturbed, overheard, observed, or intruded upon. The authority for the protection of such a sphere originates in such explicit provisions of the Constitution as the prohibition of unreasonable searches, but it has been held to derive as well from principles implicit in the Bill of Rights as a whole.

Imagine an experiment in which the state, in order to determine

47. In social experimentation the need is for prospective guidance about whether the experiment meets scientific standards in its design while in malpractice the expert is called to say whether the defendant has so far departed from professional expectations that his conduct ought not be protected, even as an acceptable, albeit unfortunate "error of judgment."

48. Gerald Gunther, "In Search of Evolving Doctrine on a Changing Court: A Model for a Newer Equal Protection," *Harvard Law Review*, vol. 86 (November 1972), pp. 8–9.

49. See, for example, *San Antonio Independent School District v. Rodriguez*, 411 U.S. 1 (1973); *Lindsey v. Normet*, 405 U.S. 56 (1972); *Richardson v. Belcher*, 404 U.S. 78 (1971); and *Dandridge v. Williams*, 397 U.S. 471 (1970).

whether a complete ban on pornography would increase or decrease the number of sex-related offenses committed, established surveillance of a random group of involuntary (and unsuspecting) subjects to determine whether they observed or purchased pornography, viewed it in their homes, and engaged in sex-related crimes. Such research would almost certainly be found to have violated the subjects' fundamental interest in privacy.[50]

When a fundamental interest is at issue, due process requires that the state's purposes, if found to be compelling, be sought by the least drastic means. If the knowledge needed to improve the laws "is impossible to obtain any other way,"[51] and the experiment has been designed so as to minimize its adverse impact on the subjects' fundamental interests, systematic experimentation is permissible. The problem for those charged with reviewing social experiments will be to determine how seriously to regard the incidental invasions of privacy caused by such experiments since a frontal assault would be exceptional.

PROBLEMS OF ENDS. Consideration of the constitutionality of government action usually means judicial review, which is unlikely to dwell for very long on the legitimacy of the ends being sought by the state. Since the mid-1930s the Supreme Court, rather than requiring the legislature to provide a rationale for its action, has repeatedly upheld statutes if it was convinced that there was any conceivable justification for them.[52]

Nevertheless, it would seem advisable that the designers of social experiments be careful that their projects have adequately articulated ends which are reasonably related to legitimate goals of the state. Moreover, the Court has on occasion been unwilling to strain its imagination to supply legitimate rationales for a neglectful government.[53] It should not be difficult for experimenters to show that the state has a legitimate interest in providing new knowledge about social interactions and in permitting "valid conclusions [to be drawn] about the relative effectiveness of various methods"[54] of distributing public services, benefits, and costs.

---

50. See Thomas I. Emerson, "The FBI and the Bill of Rights," in Pat Watters and Stephen Gillers, eds., *Investigating the FBI* (Doubleday, 1973), p. 412. See also *Katz* v. *United States*, 389 U.S. 347 (1967); *Marcus* v. *Search Warrant*, 367 U.S. 717 (1961); and *Boyd* v. *United States*, 116 U.S. 616 (1886); but see *United States* v. *White*, 401 U.S. 745 (1971).

51. Rivlin, *Systematic Thinking for Social Action*, p. 108.

52. See, for example, *Williamson* v. *Lee Optical, Inc.*, 348 U.S. 483 (1955).

53. See *James* v. *Strange*, 407 U.S. 128 (1972).

54. Rivlin, *Systematic Thinking for Social Action*, p. 87.

There is also a good argument that the state, like the scientist, has an interest in the production of knowledge for its own sake, regardless of its instrumental value.

An experiment that implicated the fundamental interests of its involuntary subjects or divided them into groups by means of a suspect classification (one drawn, for example, on racial grounds) ought almost certainly to be scrutinized carefully. It is an open question whether a desire to produce knowledge per se, perhaps even useful knowledge, would be a compelling enough interest to justify such actions. While social experiments are unlikely to provoke strict scrutiny of ends, some may interfere with basic rights, as, for example, research in the criminal law process.[55] Were a judge in sentencing a group of three hundred people of like characteristics randomly to assign sixty to a minimum security institution, sixty to the maximum allowable sentence at the ordinary prison, and the balance to individually determined sentences, would his purpose of following up their eventual readjustment to society, success, or criminal recidivism excuse his arbitrariness? The general goals of criminal punishment, of which the judge is an instrument, are incapacitation of the offender, rehabilitation, perhaps retribution, and deterrence of future crime by him or by others. Such goals are compelling enough to justify the deprivation of liberty and imposition of pain that result from criminal sanctions. But a judge is not serving these ends when testing the relative efficacy of varying dispositions (though the knowledge gained may make the other goals, of deterrence, and so on, more easily achievable in the future). Whether an experiment passes due process must be decided for each case individually. Weighed against the seriousness of the interest of the subjects that is to be compromised will be such factors as the state's need for the information to be provided by the experiment, the severity of the problems created by lack of knowledge, and perhaps the importance of the underlying legislative subject matter. It would, for example, seem improper to justify an experiment to produce information on a matter that may only remotely involve the need for state regulation.

EQUAL PROTECTION OF THE LAWS. The problem of inequality of treatment, of discrimination for or against the participants in an experi-

---

55. For examples, see Lefstein, "Experimental Research in the Law"; Freund, "Ethical Problems in Human Experimentation," pp. 687–92; and Norval Morris, "Impediments to Penal Reform," *University of Chicago Law Review,* vol. 33 (Summer 1966), pp. 646–53.

ment, is the central one raised by social experimentation.[56] Typically an experiment involves discrimination at three stages: selection of a problem for study and hence of a target population, then of a particular locale, and finally of individual subjects. The initial selection stage is peculiarly a matter of policy to be determined by persons other than the courts. The Supreme Court has found "no constitutional requirement that a regulation, in other respects permissible, must reach every class to which it might be applied."[57]

In a genuine, systematic experiment, rather than just a novel and untested program, one or more locales must be chosen from which the study population will be selected. From a scientific point of view, as well as from the viewpoint of economy and efficiency, there is every reason to select manageable subsections of the population for study. The choice of groups may depend on matters related to local government cooperation, the representativeness of particular local groups, and convenience (such as availability of necessary social science personnel and support facilities in the locality, and proximity to investigators' base of operations). Decisions reached by a legislature on the basis of such factors would very likely be sustained by the courts; such decisions made by the administrators of a social experiment, without legislative guidance, would be more vulnerable.

Unfortunately, the one example of judicial consideration of the problems of discrimination at this level of selection—*Aguayo* v. *Richardson*—seems to be based on a false analogy. The court was satisfied that the different treatment of the subjects in the two experimental groups did not run afoul of the Fourteenth Amendment. Drawing on Justice Brandeis's dissent in *New State Ice Co.* v. *Liebmann,* the judges held that just as an experiment in the "laboratory" of "a single courageous State" is permitted under the Constitution, so "the Equal Protection clause should not be held to prevent a state from conducting an experiment designed for the good of all, including the participants, on less than a statewide basis."[58] The attack on the statute in *New State,* however, was based on the alleged impropriety of a restriction that was imposed uniformly on

56. The Fourteenth Amendment explicitly requires that states not deprive anyone of "the equal protection of the laws." A similar requirement has been read into the Fifth Amendment, which is binding on federal action. *Bolling* v. *Sharpe,* 347 U.S. 497 (1954).

57. *Silver* v. *Silver,* 280 U.S. 117, 123 (1929); accord, *Williamson* v. *Lee Optical, Inc.,* 348 U.S. 483, 489 (1955).

58. *Aguayo* v. *Richardson,* 473 F.2d 1090, 1109 (2d Cir. 1973).

all Oklahomans; such restrictions in no way ran afoul of the equal protection clause, which only limits the variations that a single political en-
tity may engage in within its boundaries. Thus, the analogy between the
interstate differences that Brandeis encouraged in *New State* and the
intrastate differences upheld in *Aguayo* is a false one.

The second ground on which the *Aguayo* court found no equal protection problem posed by the New York experiments was that the selection "of certain areas of the state to try out a program for the very purpose of determining whether it, or some variation of it should be made
applicable to all" is permissible since it was "on a random but rational
basis."[59] Apparently Judge Friendly intended that the concept of "rationality" carry a great deal of freight. Typically, the courts allow "a wide
scope of discretion" to the legislator or administrator who draws a classification, disapproving only when the line is drawn "on grounds wholly
irrelevant to the achievement of the State's objective" and "despite the
fact that, in practice, [the line] result[s] in some inequality."[60] Yet the
selection of experimental subjects is purposeful, not inadvertent; such
drawing of lines *must* "result in some inequality," or perhaps a great
deal, for the experiment to provide a significant result, since it is intended
to discriminate between like groups of persons and to permit the investigators to study the results of such discrimination. Thus, approval of policy
experiments on the basis of "judicial deference" to the rationality of legislative and administrative decisions seems inappropriate, although randomness itself may still prove to be "rational" in the constitutional sense.

In the selection of individuals as subjects from among a designated
local population the potential for unfair discrimination becomes clearest,
for it obviously raises questions of equality caused by random selection.
The initial selection of a target population is the result of a policy choice,
and selection of a particular locale, while it may include randomness,
is partly a matter of policy and simple convenience. As the process of
selection narrows, it increasingly involves administrative or executive,
rather than legislative, choices. This is a particularly significant point
since the equal protection clause is not merely a philosophical statement
but one instrument among many designed to achieve fairness in governmental decisions. "Nothing opens the door to arbitrary action so effectively," as Justice Jackson observed concerning underinclusive classifications, as allowing "officials to pick and choose only a few to whom they

59. Ibid.
60. *McGowan v. Maryland*, 366 U.S. 420, 425–26 (1961).

will apply legislation and thus to escape the political retribution that might be visited upon them if larger numbers were affected."[61]

Though the issues raised in the selection of individual subjects will obviously have been present at the earlier stages, it is unlikely that the procedures will be challenged before individual subjects have been selected. Any challenge will probably turn on the burdens or benefits involved, and on the means used to include and exclude, which in this context specifically means the legitimacy of random selection.

There is no simple answer to be found in the opinions of the Supreme Court to the question of what difference in treatment can be accorded persons who are similarly situated. At the outer limit, the Court has held that the state's action must not work an "invidious" discrimination.[62] The offensiveness of a particular act must be judged on both absolute and comparative bases. On the one hand, there may be some things that it is not permissible to do to a person in the subject's situation, regardless of what is done to others—to subject him to a significant risk of death or grave injury, for example. The burden imposed on draft-age citizens during wartime must be considered outside this restriction, because if compulsory military service is not regarded as sui generis, any imposition by the state could be justified by analogy.[63] On the other hand, the fact that an action is permissible in an absolute sense would not keep it from being invidious if it were grossly out of line with the way in which others in the subject's group were treated. Norval Morris has argued, for example, that correctional research is permissible with two safeguards: first, that it take place after the judge has imposed a "just and appropriate sentence," and second, that it be guided by the principle of "less severity," which would require the experimental treatment to be no more severe than the one that would otherwise be imposed on the subject.[64] Morris is arguing for an absolute standard, set in effect in each individual case; yet the resulting distinctions between subjects and nonsubjects might still seem odious if the treatments differed substantially (for better or worse) between the two, and particularly if the nonsubjects served the experiments as controls. Where the difference between the few who are

61. *Railway Express Agency* v. *New York,* 336 U.S. 106, 112–13 (1949) (concurring opinion).

62. *Dandridge* v. *Williams,* 397 U.S. 471 (1970).

63. See Charles Black, "Constitutional Problems in Compulsory 'National Service,' " *Yale Law Report,* Summer 1967, p. 19.

64. Morris, "Impediments to Penal Reform," pp. 648 and 656.

subjected to a burden and the many who are not is great enough, the burden would be impermissible, particularly if it amounted to a punishment and were thus subject to the limitations of the cruel and unusual punishment clause of the Eighth Amendment.[65]

Whether looked at from an absolute or comparative vantage point, the invidiousness of the discrimination caused by a social experiment will probably depend on a combination of two factors: the severity of the problem for which a tentative remedy is being tested, and the extent (in value and duration) of that remedy. This applies to the exclusion of potential subjects from benefits as well as to the imposition of burdens on them. For instance, a year-long experiment to increase the average reading examination scores of a group of fifth-graders by giving each member of the group fifteen minutes of individual tutoring per week would raise fewer problems of unfairness to fifth graders excluded from the study group than would a five-year research project in which selected members of a group of elderly people with no other means of support were given an annual income of $10,000 and a rent-free apartment in a retirement village. Outside of a few polar cases, however, the prohibition on invidious discrimination does not supply much guidance, nor are many of the benefits or burdens of social experiments likely to cross over the line in any clear fashion.

Closely linked to the question of benefits and burdens is the means employed to select the groups on which they will be imposed. Indeed, a judge may determine that a classification is invidious on the ground that the selection process has been biased for or against a definable group, particularly if the group has distinct racial, religious, or ethnic characteristics since the differential treatment of such a group is itself constitutionally odious.[66] Likewise, if the burden imposed compromises a fundamental right of one group, strict scrutiny will be applied in judging the bases on which that group was selected from the total population.[67]

The large-scale social experiments that have been undertaken recently are unlikely to involve a suspect ethnic or racial classification. They may, however, impose greater burdens on the poor, for the sake of gaining

65. *Furman* v. *Georgia,* 408 U.S. 238 (1972).

66. Such classifications are regarded as "suspect" and trigger strict judicial scrutiny. *Loving* v. *Virginia,* 388 U.S. 1 (1967).

67. See *Eisenstadt* v. *Baird,* 405 U.S. 438 (1972); *Dunn* v. *Blumstein,* 405 U.S. 330 (1972). See also, Frank I. Michelman, "On Protecting the Poor Through the Fourteenth Amendment," *Harvard Law Review,* vol. 83 (November 1969), p. 36.

information about human behavior in various markets (such as labor, housing, or health care) that may be useful in formulating policy that will be beneficial to poor and nonpoor alike. The Court has described classifications based on wealth as "highly suspect,"[68] but it has never used wealth as an independent ground for invalidation.

It is possible that some social experiments could eventuate in a racially suspect division of subjects. If the judge in the hypothetical correctional experiment, for example, should attempt to measure differences by racial background, his methods of selection might seem invidious. Suppose that 210 of the 300 convicts were black and 90 were white. If 60 convicts were assigned randomly without regard to race to each experimental treatment, each would have 16 white and 44 black subjects, and there would be 58 whites and 122 blacks in the control group. If the judge attempted to match the membership of each group, 30 whites and 30 blacks would be assigned to each experimental group, and the control group would have 30 matching whites and blacks plus 120 additional blacks. Then 72 percent of the blacks would be receiving the standard disposition as opposed to 58 percent under random assignment, while 14 percent, as opposed to 21 percent, would be getting either the most or the least severe treatment. This would appear to present a clear instance of unequal treatment based on race, and it is doubtful that it would be permitted, unless there were a rational connection between race and the outcome that the experiment was intended to measure (recidivism, for instance). The point would have to be compellingly established, however, to overcome the suspicion with which racial groupings are viewed; it would not be enough that it was one of a number of ends the experiment was designed to serve. Yet for this to be the case, the initial hypothesis that the subject pool was 300 essentially similar individuals would have to be invalid, for they should properly be viewed as falling into two distinct groups.

It thus appears that random assignment in mandatory experiments is preferable to one based on certain factors. But how does it stand up against the argument that random assignment is impermissible in place of rational assignment according to constitutionally permissible criteria? In certain instances, it may be impossible to find relevant criteria that

68. *McDonald* v. *Board of Election Commissioners,* 394 U.S. 802, 807 (1969). In *Furman* v. *Georgia,* 408 U.S. 238, 242 (1972), Justice Douglas, concurring, found the death penalty to be "unusual" punishment if it discriminates by reason of "race, religion, wealth, social position, or class."

will narrow a group down to the needed size without being very socially destructive.[69] In those instances, random selection might be an acceptable means of choosing, even though the burden thus arbitrarily assigned would be very heavy (for example, death). Arguably, in experiments such as those contested in *Aguayo,* it is sufficient to answer that although the subjects bear unequal burdens, all welfare recipients in the state stood at the same ex ante risk of being selected (assuming that the court was correct that a random method was used to narrow down the subject pool).

But in the hypothetical experiment involving the three hundred convicts, the alternative of using some criteria exists. Thus, it is not possible to argue that randomness comports with equal protection because everyone has the same ex ante chance of getting a good or bad outcome. Some of the convicts, for example, would have a persuasive argument that the application of traditional criteria to their cases would mean that they would never be given the maximum sentence and that if a minimum security facility were introduced on a regular basis (rather than as part of an experiment) they would very probably be sentenced to it.[70] Thus, the equality of such a convict with the others in terms of risk under the experiment is in fact unequal to the position he could reasonably expect to have been in had there been no experiment.

The researcher's answer to this argument is that the *purpose* of the experiment is to discover whether, holding all other variables constant, the differences in disposition affect convicts' rehabilitation and so forth. There being no confidence that present criteria are relevant, only randomized assignment will permit this question to be answered; it should then be possible to develop better criteria. The researcher is arguing that in the context of an experiment, random assignment is the most rational way to distribute benefits and burdens, as Judge Friendly may have been suggesting in *Aguayo.*

Rationality is required by both the due process and equal protection clauses as a safeguard against arbitrariness. Random selection is arbitrary only in the sense that it depends on the caprice of chance; its outcome is

---

69. The allocation of very scarce life-saving therapy, such as an artificial kidney, among a group of equally needy patients is an example.

70. For that reason the validity of the experiment would be seriously compromised if enrollment were made voluntary, since the participating population would be biased toward those who evaluated their own chances of getting a better deal as being low or those who enjoyed taking risks regardless of the odds.

uncertain and unexplainable on rational grounds—indeed, that is what makes it valuable in experimentation. It is not arbitrary in the sense of being dependent on the pleasure of the person making the selection, and that is the arbitrariness that has earned a bad name in constitutional jurisprudence, for the obvious reason that persons with arbitrary power may behave despotically and may use their discretion to impose burdens unfairly and on impermissible grounds (for example, race, ethnic group, or national origin). Furthermore, unlike other kinds of arbitrary decision making, which use the cloak of discretion to frustrate review, random selection in experimentation can be reviewed; that is, a statistician can determine whether the method used did generate a random result.

Outside of experimentation, randomness seldom arises as an issue for resolution by the law. In its last incarnation the military draft was run as a lottery because the "method of random selection will provide the most equitable basis for selection of registrants for military training and service."[71] The court challenges brought against the first set of "random sequence numbers," on the ground that the December 1, 1969, drawing was biased toward the early selection of birthdays falling at the end of the year, resulted in apparent (but at most indirect) acceptance of the use of a lottery.[72] But rules relating to military service may not be applicable in other situations; moreover, the lottery may have been used here because the necessary winnowing could not otherwise be accomplished without causing greater inequities and unacceptable legal and societal ramifications.

The other occasion that courts have had to consider random allocation also involved a burden that was very different from any that could be expected in social policy experimentation—the death penalty. In holding the death penalty to be cruel and unusual punishment in *Furman* v. *Georgia*,[73] the Supreme Court did not reverse its earlier holding in *McGautha* v. *California* that the power to impose that sentence could be committed "to the untrammeled discretion of the jury" without guidelines or restrictions.[74] But it did seem to be agreeing with Justice Brennan's dissent in *McGautha* that the majority provided "no mechanism

71. Presidential Proclamation, Nov. 26, 1969.
72. *Stodolsky* v. *Hershey*, 2 S.S.L.R. 3527 (W.D. Wisc. 1969), and *United States* v. *Kotrlik & Gaevert*, 5 S.S.L.R. 3693 (9th Cir. 1972).
73. 408 U.S. 238 (1972). For the equal protection reasoning of *Furman* to come into play in judging a social policy experiment, the burdens of the experiment would have to fall unevenly on a particular identifiable group.
74. 402 U.S. 183, 196 (1971).

to prevent . . . consciously maximized variation from reflecting merely random or arbitrary choice."[75] In *Furman* the Court recognized that standardless decisions made in private can be arbitrary in reflecting the deliberate choice of twelve jurors to punish more severely members of a group drawn on constitutionally impermissible grounds. A number of the justices went further and concluded that "merely random" choices are objectionable. Justice Stewart, for example, found that "death sentences are cruel and unusual in the same way that being struck by lightning is cruel and unusual."[76]

To the extent that the constitutional law applicable in the death cases would carry weight in social experiments, it would appear that the imposition of the burdens of an experiment on "a capriciously selected random handful"[77] would be unconstitutional. The analogy seems strained, however, and the reasoning at least counterbalanced by the arguments favoring randomness as the means of selection in social policy experiments. It is true that random assignment prevents predictability, which may be important to subjects; it may also be employed when the choice is hardest to make, so that the disparity between those chosen and those not is greatest in terms of proportion and of burden and benefit. Yet, if there really are no valid grounds for dividing the initial group, randomness has the advantage of being evenhanded and rationally related to the state's (and investigator's) interest in conducting a valid experiment.

75. Ibid., 248.
76. *Furman* v. *Georgia,* 408 U.S. 238, 309 (1972) (concurring opinion).
77. Ibid., 248, note 11.

THOMAS C. SCHELLING

General Comments

The issues that social scientists get concerned about seem to depend on the kinds of social experiments they have in mind—on the experiments they happen to be engaged in, or were recently subjected to, or have often wished they might perform.

The large-scale social experiments discussed at this conference have some specialized characteristics. They are protracted, academically designed, and federally financed. Their subjects are individuals who are identified ahead of time and kept track of, and who know that they are in the experiment. And the experiments involve amounts of money or changes in behavior that are far from trivial.

They furthermore involve no actions or decisions on the part of the subjects that are shocking or even novel. The subjects are not chosen because they have a particular interest in the outcome or in the policies that may be based on the results of the experiment. And, with the possible exception of intrafamily relations, the scope of activities affected by the experiments does not include the relations of subjects to each other or their relations with people who are not part of the experiment and who gave no consent. (The subjects do not have to become experimenters themselves in dealing with, recruiting, deceiving, or otherwise behaving insincerely with either friends or strangers.)

In contrast, one can imagine experiments in which nobody even knows who the subjects are. Something may be randomly broadcast, or noise may be randomly introduced into some broadcast or widespread communications activity; there is an observed statistical increase in some frequency, but nobody knows—neither the experimenter nor the subject—who actually was targeted. Testing response to a doubling of the frequency of wrong numbers in the telephone system might be an example. Then there are the experiments—say, with traffic-regulating systems—in which the affected subjects know who they are but the experimenters do not, as well as experiments in which the experimenters know but the subjects do not.

A Typology of Social Experiments

There is not, as yet, a typology, or set of classifying characteristics, by which to describe particular experiments and contrast them with other experiments. The degree of identification of the subjects—to the experimenters, to themselves individually, or to each other as a group—might be one important characteristic.

The question whether the subjects are in some sense an organized group could be important. At one extreme the subjects could be a group that was already organized, had procedures for reaching collective decisions, had good internal communication, and was even so integral a group that it could officially communicate. Perhaps it has procedures for giving collective consent, or for negotiating the terms of an experiment and policing commitments made to the group as subjects. At the other extreme an experimental group could be one in which no one affected would ever know who else had been affected or how to get in touch with any others.

Another classifying dimension is the way in which participants will be reported on in the study. Much of the discussion of whether it is politically dangerous or humanly undignified to be looked at, studied, identified by name, and so on, is pertinent or not according to whether the subject could ever be identified individually—whether he might be subjected to interrogation by the police or the Internal Revenue Service or narcotics agents because of information provided through the study. My impression is that some people do mind and some people do not mind acting roles as long as they are masked, anonymous, behaving as they have been asked to behave and not being themselves. Indeed there may be at least three kinds of people: those whose sense of personal identity and integrity is so strong that no amount of anonymity can keep them from feeling personally violated if their intimate activities or thoughts are captured and recorded; those who don't care as long as anonymity is assured; and those who positively adore confiding intimate personal information as long as their identities will be protected.

Another characteristic of experiments is immediately suggested. By what criteria may the subjects screen themselves without spoiling the sample? If some people need protection, can't tolerate scrutiny, feel uncomfortable when participating, lack trust in the experimenters, or would be personally embarrassed to take money for participating, while others feel that being paid to participate in an experiment is at least as dignified, intrudes no more in their private lives, and yields no more intimate information about them than the jobs they already hold and the lives they already lead, can some kind of screening or self-selection limit participation to the latter group without spoiling the experiment? With some experiments the answer is sure to be no, and with others the answer ought to be a good deal more favorable.

An important aspect is the question of who uses the information. There are surely social experiments in which the primary users of the information are the subjects themselves, who discover by collective experimental action that certain kinds of collective actions pay. They go on using or not using the system they experimented with, because it was mainly for their benefit. An experiment in traffic control at a football stadium, if the configuration of roads and parking lots is peculiar to the particular stadium at which the experiment is performed, is primarily designed so that the subjects may discover a better system than the one they had been struggling with. Or, if the results of the experiment can be generalized to other traffic situations at other stadiums, the subjects may still have benefited enough to have a collective interest in performing the experiment (even though they might prefer to use the results at some other stadium, if it is going to take several tries to find a system that works). But there is the important case in which a group of people collectively decide to experiment on themselves. If a small sample is to be chosen, and if the experiment is onerous, then theirs is the ethical problem; and if such a group accepts the help of an experimenter who hopes to use the information for wider application, he may not need to impose his ethics on them.

Far different is the kind of experiment that is designed to gather information that is bound to be used against the subject population. It may be an experiment designed to control pilferage in a place of business, littering by passersby, smoking by teenagers, driving by people without licenses, playing hooky from school, purchasing contraband, breaking the speed laws. Unless the target population is so tightly organized it can police its own agreement to boycott the experiment, it may not be hard to induce some part of the population, even all of the population, to participate for compensation, even though there is a group interest in denying the information that is being sought. This one characteristic cannot come close to determining what the ethics ought to be, but it does seem to be one important characteristic of social experiments.

Another possibly interesting characteristic is the degree of urgency or concentration of interest in the experiment. There are some experiments in which the degree of intrusion or interference or risk to the subjects is highly concentrated, being individually large while the number of individuals is small; the benefits of the experiment are diffuse, widespread, thinly distributed, and perhaps never even noticed by the beneficiaries who, enormous in number, enjoy some large benefit in the aggregate. But the opposite case can occur. The experiment may involve a very large number of people, to whom the nuisance or intrusion is small, while the benefits may be measured in the avoidance of utter disaster by a tiny group of beneficiaries, known or unknown. Experiments with alternative airport-facilities design and inspection procedures that are not only a nuisance but possibly an intrusion into the privacy of tens or hundreds of thousands of people might produce results that eventually would be used to reduce the likelihood of a single airplane disaster.

Closely related may be a general suspicion of academically designed experiments. It is part of the academic culture that knowledge has value for its own sake; truth is not always measured by its market value or instrumental utility; controversies are worth resolving with evidence, even if no public policy hinges on them. There may be a certain suspicion that scientists and other academic people have a strong amateur interest in the kind of knowledge that a social experiment will generate—perhaps an experiment that asks some sacrifice or public-spirited participation by subjects who are not adequately compensated in material goods. There may be some who have, or think they have, grounds for considering this unfair and even deceptive. It may be argued that there ought to be some degree of urgency in the public use of experimental results before people are recruited through any means other than straightforward hiring. But it should equally be kept in mind that there may well be urgent situations in which the interest in experimental results is not at all academic. If the problem is to devise schemes for coping with a severe shortage of heating oil this winter, with a shortage of flu vaccine, with terrorist bombs in public places, or with school busing, it may well be judged that the stakes in the experimental results are of the same order of importance as the potential hazards and costs and improprieties in the experiment itself. There ought to be some way to judge the inhibitions on experimentation by reference to the urgency and seriousness of the problem to whose solution the experiment is expected to make a contribution.

Finally, an important characteristic of many of these experiments is that there exist, within the context of the experiment, some strong presumptions about ethical rules, standards, traditions, and fair play. Consider a social experiment in offtrack betting. The notion of what is fair compensation to somebody who placed his bet and lost would probably be very different from the notion of what is fair about selling some novel kind of insurance to an illiterate. There is an ethic, a tradition; an understanding of what is fair in a betting parlor is not the same as what is fair in a parking lot. Often the context will suggest certain appropriate currencies for compensation, and rule out others. An experiment in a hospital that wanted to provide compensation for children who might be harmed would often be looked at askance if the hospital said it had plenty of money and offered to make a handsome cash settlement if a child lost his left arm. But if the hospital were to say it had excellent health facilities and, if anything went wrong, not only would the child get the best treatment possible but, as compensation, be a favored patient for the rest of his life, this insurance policy that paid off not in cash but in hospital services might be considered appropriate. (Its appropriateness would have nothing to do with whether the child, or his parents, or the child after he grew up, would far prefer cash in some amount that would save the hospital money.) Notice that one difference here may be in providing compensation directly to the child rather than to his parents.

While I think that too high a price is often paid to disguise the nature of compensation, and too little advantage taken of the fact that money is highly acceptable in return for unexpected shocks and losses, it is nevertheless often the case that one can identify some peculiarly appropriate, acceptable, legitimate currency that is specific to the context of the particular experiment.

Another important characteristic of any one of these social experiments may be the answer to the question: what is the alternative? There are surely some experiments to which the alternative is simply to forget it —not do it, forgo the opportunity. But for a good many social experiments there are at least two significant alternatives, alternatives whose consideration ought to help determine whether or not to proceed in spite of some ethical reservations.

One of these alternatives is simply to proceed with an important decision without the knowledge that the experiment might have provided.

In medicine, this may mean administering doses on guesswork rather than on experimentation. In other contexts it may mean relying on guesswork in designing traffic controls, instituting school lunches, allotting housing space or assigning office space, zoning a city, rationing heating fuel, abolishing or generalizing team teaching in third grade, or whatever it might be toward which the experiment was intended to provide either a better basis for judging whether or not to proceed, or a better basis for designing the system, choosing its scale or intensity, or identifying special cases and special hazards in advance so that people could be alert to safeguards and necessary screening procedures.

The other alternative is sometimes, but not always, nearly the same thing: to go ahead and initiate the program, but less gradually, and with less overt attention to learning in the early stages how to redesign the program in the later stages. Most publicly financed policy-oriented social experiments are simply programs that were going to be inaugurated anyway, but that were carefully and consciously initiated with enough experimental design and enough facilities for observation and quick feedback so that the early stages of the program could be utilized as an experiment, even though the program would have gone ahead in the absence of any experimental self-consciousness. Actually, designing the early stages of a program for experimental use is frequently a conservative approach, one that emphasizes the virtue of gradualism, that leaves more options open, that admits the possibility of error and the need for modification. In this context the difference between experiment and experience is mainly in the systematic way that experiences are generated and observed and analyzed. If somebody proposed experimenting with preventive detention of people with certain mental diseases, or Christmas leave for convicts serving life terms, or methadone maintenance, or vocational rehabilitation of former convicts, or wrong-way high-speed express-bus lanes on the freeways, the alternative to the experiment is likely to be just rushing ahead without consciously designed procedures to evaluate performance, to preserve useful information, to take advantage of experimental design, and to discern details that could help to reshape the program.

Or the alternative might be just to do nothing at all, on grounds that without a trial balloon you wouldn't dare send up a balloon with passengers. And if it is unethical to do it with a trial balloon, you will never know whether lifers let out to have Thanksgiving dinner with their families would nearly always return on Sunday or instead would nearly always steal a car and head for the Mexican border.

Consent

In the profession of economics, how to impute a preference to a collection of individuals who are not in complete agreement is generally considered to be a difficult, elusive, subtle theoretical problem. The award of the Nobel Prize in Economics to Kenneth Arrow publicized the problem of how to tell when a group consents. Worse, it publicized a theorem to the effect that there may be no rule that can ever be devised, no rule that conforms to all intuitively attractive criteria and violates no intuitively attractive criteria, for telling when a group of people has something that might be called a group preference or is able to make an unambiguous collective choice.

Politically the question can always be settled by a vote. Or an elected representative can consult an oracle. Or a variety of compromise techniques can be used to force at least grudging consent. But it is extraordinarily hard to decide whether 10,000 people have consented when 4,000 have said yes, 3,000 no, 2,000 that they don't know, 500 that they don't care, and a few that they protest the procedure and won't answer.

The problem need not arise if only individual consent is needed. If in a city there are 100,000 eligible people and among them 10,000 will be suitable subjects for an experiment, it makes no difference whether another 90,000 would not like to have been coerced into the experiment by a majority vote. They don't have to be coerced into it. But there are at least two circumstances in which it may be necessary to include some who don't want to be included. The most obvious case is that in which some group that has a prior definition, like all the residents of a particular territory or building, or all the people who find themselves in a theater or on an airplane, must perforce be in the experiment. Experimenting with a speed limit, music at the shopping mall, integration of first and second grades, or daylight saving time cannot easily be confined to those who consent, the rest of the local population being excused. Nor can dissenters be excluded when statistical design requires a sample that ought not to be biased by self-selection for the experiment.

Brown suggests that the community consent for an experiment could be decided by majority rule. That may be satisfactory, but only if there are no significant ethical considerations involved, and no serious disproportions in the way the experiment affects different people who, whether they like it or not, end up participating. If 10,000 school children are going to be experimented on with high-cholesterol lunches, tobacco and marijuana and placebo cigarettes, or uniformed policemen in the school corridors, the decision may have to turn on whether or not 5,000 parents, or some more commanding number, say yes. But this should probably not be referred to as "consent."

For large-scale social experiments, unless subjects can be brought in through some market mechanism, it is unlikely that any group with a prior definition will ever be quite unanimous in its consent—or unanimous without what some commentators have been calling "undue inducements." (Or, as probably happens, a majority coerces the minority to shut up and sign up, or a minority coerces the majority to do so.)

A special case of nonconsent is worth noticing also. That is one in which the subjects have an adverse interest in the experiment itself— would like to block it—not because they object to being experimented on but because they don't want that kind of knowledge to be gathered. Suppose someone is going to experiment with a system of rewards for anonymous tips on stealing, or smoking marijuana in the high school. Suppose the experiment were going to be used to improve techniques of catching and apprehending, perhaps trapping, some of the children. Like the objections to a study known as Camelot a decade ago, there may be objections to the political and administrative motives behind the experiment itself. In that case, letting the minority be outvoted by a majority may be either right or wrong, but the result can hardly be called "consent."

Difficult as it may be to decide what constitutes consent for an individual, and especially for an individual who is physically or mentally incapable of informed consent, there is a general problem, to which no solution has ever been found and probably no satisfactory solution ever can be found, in interpreting the notion of consent for a group of people who disagree (or who may express agreement only because of internal coercion).

Compensation

Many issues arise with respect to appropriate compensation for subjects. But there is one aspect of compensation in social experiments that is very different from compensation in most private experiments, which test something other than behavior.

Most medical experiments are not mainly concerned with behavior, or with the influence of inducements on behavior. True, there are experiments with placebos that would be spoiled if ethics required that the patient receiving a placebo be told that it was a placebo. There are probably experiments on reactions to pain that wouldn't work if pain had to be suppressed by anesthesia so that nobody could suffer during the experiment. But for most medical experiments the motivation of the patient is not central to the experiment. If one can eliminate risk, anxiety, even the patient's awareness of what the choices are, one does not thereby eliminate what is central to the experiment but something incidental to it, and often something that may detract as much as contribute. One still has to worry that financial inducements may bring a nonrandom sample of the population into the experiment, because the thing to be experimented on is somehow correlated with the willingness of people to participate for money. But by and large a medical experiment is not spoiled by the nature of the arrangements for reassurance and compensation.

Many social experiments, including the recent large-scale experiments, are focused exactly on the question: How will individuals or groups react to changes in incentives, in risks, in different modes of compensation, in the restructuring of the options and alternatives available? It is impossible to take the risk out of an experiment in risk-taking without spoiling the experiment. Nor can money compensation be eliminated from an experiment if the experiment is designed to test responses to money compensation.

In other words, many of these social experiments are precisely focused on incentives, on decisions under uncertainty, on reactions to risk, and on other choices that have financial consequences. If an experiment were designed to take care of all the risks, to equalize all the compensations, to eliminate the uncertainties, and to assure people that they can never regret the choices they made because it will all be evened out in the end, then not simply the pain and the risk and the uncertainty would be eliminated, but the experiment would be left out of the experiment.

We might offer a person who is given a new vaccine the possibility of extraordinary compensation if he contracts some terrible fever, and then discover that either psychosomatically or through skulduggery he contracts a fever, takes the money, and spoils the results. But in this case it is at least possible to go to work to try to design out of the experiment the ability to contract an artificial fever, or to graduate the money compensation so that the fever is not worth it, or even to make sure that the fever is bad enough that nobody would be tempted to incur it to win a money prize. None of these changes would spoil the experiment. But if this were an experiment to see how much money it took to get somebody to contract a fever artificially, it would be a different kind of problem.

People who deprecate "undue enticement" are somewhat like those who explain that paying household help too much spoils them. Considering the things that people are hired to do every day—demeaning things and dishonest things and disagreeable things and risky things—considering even how many people are hired for experiments within a place of business, concern that the subject of an experiment might risk his life or health for money, or sell away some of his dignity and privacy for money, seems misplaced. People incur risks of life and health and sell away privacy and dignity every day in every country of the world. If the designers of an experiment have worked responsibly and conscientiously, maybe it isn't up to them to decide that in the interest of their potential subjects they should keep the compensation down. I think the notion that compensation ought to be kept low is usually arrogantly paternalistic, although sometimes it looks more like an exercise of classical oligopoly in keeping down the cost of experiments by having an ethical constraint on price competition.

The problem of compensating the subjects in the social experiments often cannot be solved by overcompensating them. If incentives are not part of the experiment, by all means overcompensate. But if incentives are at the heart of the experiment, overcompensating spoils the experiment in exactly the same way that anesthesia spoils the experiment in response to pain.

Two things have been discussed that may be useful as last resorts. One is providing insurance against any catastrophe that is beyond the order of magnitude of things the experiment is designed to measure. The other is providing lump-sum payments in advance that, being constants rather than variables in the experiment, ought to have no effect on anybody's decisions.

Can either of these techniques be insulated from the subjects' behavior? Any compensation scheme can set up incentives to beat the system. (I think one of the reasons people are reluctant to experiment on children is that children are smart; they find out how the system works and arrange to qualify for some of that delectable "undue compensation.") If subjects are given more than adequate insurance against catastrophe, they may accept the challenge and go to work on the catastrophe.

The lump sum in advance sounds fine as long as everybody is as coolly calculating as economists would have them be. But I have known even economists who, on a trip, spent exactly the amount they were allowed for travel expenses, even though that amount was fixed so that they could keep any savings if they spent less. It is difficult to give people lump sums that will compensate them if things go badly, and be a gratuitous windfall if things go well, without their carrying, even unconsciously, some notion that they have specific insurance against the contingency.

The overadequate lump sum paid in advance is better, however, than an agreement merely to make up any financial loss, if reaction to the prospect of financial loss is what the experiment is about. It covers the possibility of differential loss but arranges the zero point so that even the loss leaves the subjects ahead of where they would have been. They can react to the differential, but the differential is so high that they cannot be net losers from the experiment. It is a clever solution, and probably often a pretty good solution. But the fact that it ought not to contaminate the experiment doesn't mean that it won't.

Ethics for the Protection of Whom or What?

Most of the discussion about ethics, procedures, and rules is oriented toward the *subjects* of the experiment, and particularly toward protecting them from risk, indignity, or any consequences of which they might not be fully informed and aware and about which they might not be capable of making a responsible decision. But in most experiments on people—even in these social experiments—the ethics and the rules and procedures have very little to do with the welfare of the subjects; they have much more to do with the ethics of the profession that is involved.

This is dramatically clear with respect to medical experiments. Consider the question of whether charity patients ought to be considered to be more available to be experimented on than people who are paying their own way in a hospital, or the question whether high prices can be offered to people who allow themselves, perhaps with a compelling need to buy alcohol or narcotics, to be used for some demeaning experiment. Consider the question whether a physician experimenting on a subject who, fully alert, has agreed to the conditions of the experiment ought in the event things go badly to treat the person as a patient rather than as a subject.

A strong case can be made that a physician should never approach a sick person, medicine in hand, knife in hand, dietary regimen in hand, with any experiment in mind, in any mood or frame of mind other than the mood or frame of mind with which he typically tries to heal the sick. To emphasize the point: no practicing physician should engage in vivisection, even of animals, except possibly in an atmosphere almost reminiscent of a hospital ward. Why? Not because I care about his victims. I care about him, and the fact that he might be my physician someday. It is not easy for a person to carry around two different sets of attitudes toward human beings and human lives and human suffering, switching one off and the other on the way he would switch the lights off as he leaves the hospital ward and turn the lights on in his laboratory. A professional body has similar difficulty in maintaining two sets of ethical rules, one to govern its high-minded practice of the art of healing and comfort to the suffering, and another tough one that it takes into the experimental laboratory. Part of this has to do with the psychology of the individual, part with the sociology of rules, norms, standards, and ethics.

The primary reason for having high, even deliberately excessive, ethical standards in medical experimentation may not be to save the subjects but to save the ethics of the medical profession. And though the principle may not apply with equal force in some of the more innocuous though expensive social experiments, the ethical standards they follow are probably aimed at protecting the ethics of the profession, not protecting the subjects in the marketplace, who might be happy to hire themselves out for experimentation.

For most professional bodies, and probably for most individuals, the ethics that apply to subjects and the ethics that apply to clients and colleagues and publications are integral and nonseparable. (It is hard to be cruel to prisoners, I should guess, without becoming less considerate of people who are not prisoners.)

Many rules, especially those devised to govern professional behavior, have a ritual and conventional significance. Even the notion about the dignity of an experimental subject may have more to do with the experimenter's dignity, or the experimenter's concept of the dignity that must be imputed to the subject, or that the subject ought to have, than any real dignity of the subject that the experimenter feels obliged to preserve. Protecting the supposed rights of some experimental subjects may be a way of asserting something about the rights that the experimenter thinks everybody should have, that ought to be respected, and that he wants to protect for himself. The fact that there are subjects who don't care may be much more of a menace than an opportunity; and it may be the experimenter, his profession, and even his culture that he is protecting, not the subject, by limiting his willingness to let the subject erode his ethical practices.

To speculate even further, I suggest that where privacy and dignity and some other nonmaterial rights and interests of the subjects are concerned, experimenters are often groping not for the ethics that should constrain their experimental thrust, but rather the ethics that they wish the subjects would observe in the interest of human dignity and privacy.

Experiments as Precedents

Suppose an experiment tries something that has never been done before. Never again will it "never have been done before." In experimenting with state lotteries, offtrack betting, abortion clinics, racial integration, drug abuse, and other controversial practices, the mere fact that these things have been done, even in an experiment, makes the world a different place.

Furthermore, social experiments may prove far more than what the experiment is about. All kinds of myths may fall aside when organized crime fails to take over church bingo, or girls and boys are mixed in the classroom rather than separated between the left and right sides. Experimenting with an eighteen-year drinking age, rather than twenty-one, may not only disprove some things that some people would rather not see disproved, but it changes the base point. There was presumption that the drinking age was twenty-one, unless there was strong reason to the contrary. The experiment may move the presumed age to eighteen unless there is strong reason to the contrary. The experiment is part of history, not something in another world. You can't experiment by admitting women to a formerly male college, preserving an option to draw negative conclusions and go back to where you started as though nothing had happened.

Suppose a group of convicts got together in a prison and decided that there might be just as much deterrence if confinement were replaced by pain. Alternatively, there might be as much deterrence if confinement were replaced by capital punishment. It might be much cheaper to kill a fraction of them, or to punish them cruelly, and let the survivors go. Suppose they requested that a lottery determine some appropriate fraction among them to die so that the rest could go free, or were prepared to sign a contract that in the event they were apprehended again and convicted again they would waive their rights to anything short of capital punishment. Quite aside from whether or not this is a good and proper proposal to take under advisement, I would allege that it could not be an "experiment." That is, if this is tried, its very trial becomes an event that throws a long shadow on the course of future history. It may matter very little whether some small number of convicts suffer or gain in the trial of these schemes; it matters enormously whether or not the state does something that theretofore was considered beyond bounds.

Experiments versus Ethics

There is one place in which the interests of social experimenters and the interests of people concerned about ethics are at odds. It is a place like this conference, where the ethics of social experimentation are explored and debated, where some people are professionally involved and some intrigued by the puzzles and attracted by the conversational quality of the subject, and where most of the participants are not conscious of any legislative responsibility for whatever may come out of such a symposium.

The reason the interests are at odds is that the exploration of ethics tends to focus on the deep, the serious, the hard, the sensitive, the constitutional issues—the dangers that are possible but not those that are common—issues involving human dignity, privacy, and the obligations of sophisticated experimenters to people who, possibly because they are poor and comparatively uneducated, may be presumed, perhaps paternalistically, to be unable to watch out for themselves. In the exploration of the topics, extreme cases are posed, instances that prove the possibility of an issue, not its frequency.

In the ordinary world of experimentation, the danger may be that enthusiasts, interested primarily in their experiments or in the benefits that may result from the experiments if all goes well, may be too little attentive to some potential consequences to their subjects, or to the ethical interests of their own colleagues and of the larger society of which they are a part. Perhaps confident that there is no real danger, and harboring no ulterior motives, the experimenter may be too little sympathetic with ethical rules and inhibitions that may be superfluous to the case at hand but that cannot survive with any force if everybody feels morally justified in making his own exceptions. The person who parks his car in front of a fire hydrant in order to use a glass telephone booth, from which he can keep a lookout for fire engines and be out of their way in plenty of time in case of fire, is probably guilty of undermining an important precautionary rule, even if he is creating no immediate hazard. So may it be with experimenters who meticulously guard the interests of their subjects, and believe that that discharges any responsibility they may have toward the preservation or creation of ethical standards.

In a conference focused on ethics, and on the hazards that ethics are to guard against or even the social attitudes that ethical standards are intended to support and display, the bias is likely to be against the experiment. I cannot say "typically," because these conferences are too infrequent to permit such generalization; but they probably will not have at their disposal quantitative estimates of the frequency with which the problems arise that the ethical standards are intended to guard against, or even the particular kinds of experiments that do or do not raise ethical issues that ordinary law and conscience cannot handle. In the exploratory stage of a subject like this it is important that practical judgment not be allowed into the process too early, for it can discourage the imaginative ideas and wide-ranging analogies that help to illuminate the problems and issues. In these early stages of exploration, the danger is that the infrequent, the improbable, and the unfamiliar may get too little attention because they go unnoticed.

But if a little dramatic license is a good thing early in the exploration, the discipline of practical judgment should be brought in before conclusions are reached. Most social experiments appear to me to be almost completely innocuous. Just as it is important, in straightening out legal principles, to be clear not only about whether a murderer may legally inherit his victim's wealth if the victim's will says that he shall, but about the reasons for reaching the one conclusion or the other, it may be important to think about comparable conflicts of interest and conflicts of principle in social experimentation. But it may be equally important to avoid establishing any widespread presumption that when a man is killed his heirs must have done it, or if he died in his sleep his heirs should be presumed to have poisoned him for his wealth.

The innocuous social experiments are those that quickly come to mind —those that I bitterly wish might be performed every time I feel the victim of negligence or mismanagement in the way an airport or a parking lot is run, or automobile safety features are tested, or the sizes and furniture arrangements of conferences are decided on. I shall be sorry if either the ingenuity or the deep moral concern evident in the Brookings conferees' consideration of ethical and legal issues should cause a widespread feeling of alarm about social experiments, unless the particular kinds of social experiments about which alarm is justified are carefully defined and communicated.

Conference Participants

with their affiliations at the time of the conference

Henry J. Aaron *Brookings Institution*

Jodie T. Allen *Urban Institute*

Bernard Barber *Barnard College*

Peter G. Brown *Battelle Seattle Research Center*

Lewis Butler *U.S. Department of Health, Education, and Welfare*

Alexander Morgan Capron *University of Pennsylvania Law School*

Rashi Fein *Harvard University*

Charles Field *U.S. Department of Housing and Urban Development*

Leonard Goodwin *Brookings Institution*

Edward M. Gramlich *Brookings Institution*

Robert W. Hartman *Brookings Institution*

David N. Kershaw *Mathematica, Inc.*

William A. Klein *University of California at Los Angeles*

William A. Morrill *U.S. Department of Health, Education, and Welfare*

Joseph P. Newhouse *Rand Corporation*

Guy H. Orcutt *Yale University*

Larry L. Orr *U.S. Department of Health, Education, and Welfare*

John L. Palmer *U.S. Department of Health Education, and Welfare*

181

John A. Pincus *Rand Corporation*

Henry W. Riecken *University of Pennsylvania School of Medicine*

Alice M. Rivlin *Brookings Institution*

Thomas C. Schelling *Harvard University*

Charles L. Schultze *Brookings Institution*

Richard Shore *U.S. Department of Labor*

Daniel M. Singer *Fried, Frank, Harris, Shriver and Kampelman*

P. Michael Timpane *Brookings Institution*

Robert M. Veatch *Institute of Society, Ethics and the Life Sciences*

Harold W. Watts *University of Wisconsin*

Index of Cases Cited

General Index